30 Meals/

30 Minutes

ALSO BY JOANNA M. LUND

The Healthy Exchanges Cookbook
HELP: The Healthy Exchanges Lifetime Plan
The Diabetic's Healthy Exchanges Cookbook
Cooking Healthy with a Man in Mind
The Best of Healthy Exchanges Food Newsletter '92 Cookbook
Notes of Encouragement
It's Not a Diet, It's a Way of Life (audiotape)

30 Meals/

30 Minutes

A HEALTHY EXCHANGES® COOKBOOK

JoAnna M. Lund

HELPing Others HELP Themselves
the **Healthy Exchanges®** Way™

A Perigee Book

A Perigee Book
Published by The Berkley Publishing Group
200 Madison Avenue
New York, NY 10016

For more information about Healthy Exchanges products, contact:
Healthy Exchanges, Inc.
P.O. Box 124
DeWitt, Iowa 52742-0124
(319) 659-8234

Perigee Special Sales edition: January 1997
ISBN: 0-399-52323-5
Published simultaneously in Canada.

The Putnam Berkley World Wide Web site address is
http://www.berkley.com/berkley

Printed in the United States of America

10   9   8   7   6   5   4   3

Before using the recipes and advice in this book, consult your physician or health
provider to be sure they are appropriate for you. The information in this book is not
intended to take the place of any medical advice. It reflects the author's experiences,
studies, research, and opinions regarding a healthy lifestyle. All material included in
this publication is believed to be accurate. The publisher assumes no responsibility for
any health, welfare, or subsequent damage that might be incurred from use of these
materials.

This cookbook is dedicated to everyone at QVC and to all their loyal viewers. I felt from the first time I appeared live stirring up my "common folk" healthy recipes that Healthy Exchanges and QVC would be a great match, because we both believe in quality and value. I hope you'll agree that no recipes could be more convenient—the third element in Q-V-C—than my quick and delicious choices in this volume.

Contents

Acknowledgments

Anyone who thinks that writing and testing three cookbooks in three months is a "piece of cake"—no matter how easy to prepare the recipes are—needs to think again! It took a lot of teamwork to get this project completed on time. For being members of the Healthy Exchanges Team, I want to thank:

John Duff and Barbara O'Shea from Putnam and Amy Rosen and Paula Piercy from QVC, for cooking up the idea in the first place.

Angela Miller and Coleen O'Shea, for assuring me I could do it.

Shirley Morrow for typing, retyping, and typing again as I changed my mind on what I wanted to include.

Rita Ahlers and Gerry Stamp, for helping me test the recipes.

Janis Jackson and Susan Williams, for doing all those dishes, and I do mean *dishes*, when well over three hundred recipes had to be tested.

Lori Hansen, for lending a hand with the Food Processor II software so the recipes could be as accurate as possible in calories and grams.

Rose Hoenig, R.D., L.D., for calculating the Diabetic Exchanges.

Barbara Alpert, for helping me get my manuscript "ready for the presses" more quickly than I could have alone.

Cliff Lund, my "Official Taste Tester." His taste buds are the "Barometer of America." If he loves it, you can bet your family, your friends, and your neighbors will love it too! And he really loves the recipes in this collection of cookbooks.

The entire Healthy Exchanges crew for giving Cliff a hand with the taste-testing responsibilities.

God, for giving me the ability to create "common folk" healthy recipes. It truly is miraculous what happens when we change our prayers from what we want to what we need.

30 Meals/
30 Minutes

No Time to Cook? There's Still Time to Eat Healthy! or "Healthy" in a Hurry

It's 5:00 P.M.—or, even worse, nearly 6:00—when you hurry into the house from a day of working, shopping, carpooling, running errands, *whatever*. Everyone wants to know: "What's for dinner?" Who could blame you for ordering pizza, or piling the kids into the car for a quick trip to the nearest fast-food restaurant?

That's okay for once in a while, but too often quick-and-easy food is hard both on your waistline and your pocketbook. You'd prefer to offer your family healthy, good-tasting food every day, but is there time in your busy life to do what it takes?

I'm here to tell you that there *is*. I know exactly how it feels to juggle work and school and family, and *still* manage to find time to prepare delicious meals as part of your busy schedule. I've done it, managed to lose 130 pounds along the way—and kept it off now for six years!

My own success, which made it possible for me to help so many others, came because I finally understood that healthy eating didn't require hours in the kitchen, a hefty bank account, or a personal chef. My philosophy soon became clear: **"If it takes longer to cook it than eat it, forget it!"**

I got tired of sweating for ages over a hot stove, then finding myself with a sinkful of dirty dishes five minutes after the food hit the table. There had to be a better way, and I was determined to find it. Working from my tiny test kitchen in DeWitt, Iowa, I figured out ways to make traditional family recipes healthy—and make them *fast!* Now that the food manufacturers have jumped onto the Health Wagon with us, we can select from the best-quality reduced fat and low-sugar convenience foods, add just the right amounts of fresh fruits, vegetables, meats, and dairy products, and produce meals that taste as good as they look!

My "common folk" healthy recipes are always low in sugar and fat, prepared from ingredients found in any small-town market, and perfect for diabetics, heart patients, and anyone concerned about weight loss or lowering cholesterol. But the ones I've selected for this volume are my "quickest of the quick," and I promise you'll find lots of great ideas for feeding your family fast—and healthy too!

You'll find that these menus are generally planned to feed four or six people, meaning that the main dish and accompaniments yield that number of servings. But you'll also see that many of my desserts serve eight, and that's on purpose: it's always nice to have extra goodies on hand in the fridge or freezer to offer when unexpected company drops by!

Think about it—a month's worth of menus* you can put on the table in thirty minutes or less. Now doesn't that make the tension in your shoulders disappear?

Jo Anna

---

*I've organized this book into menus, but I want you to feel free to choose what you like from any of them and design your own favorite groupings. Remember, healthy eating only works when you eat what you enjoy.

Six Tips for Making Quick Recipes Even Quicker

1. Purchase prechopped vegetables. Yes, already chopped fresh broccoli may cost you more, but you have *no* waste and save valuable time because you don't have to chop it yourself.

2. When cooking rice or pasta, always plan to cook extra and freeze the leftovers in two-cup portions. Then, whenever you need cooked macaroni for a quick main dish, all you have to do is thaw it in the microwave while you are browning the meat in a skillet.

3. When chopping onions or green peppers, chop several at once and freeze in half-cup portions. Frozen chopped fresh vegetables thaw in moments when browned with meat. (Take advantage of seasonal sales on produce or late-day specials at farm stands. If red peppers are usually $3.99 per pound and you spot them at half price, buy a bundle—then chop and freeze!)

4. Hard-boil six eggs at the same time. When they are cooled, mark each egg with a big **H** using a marker and store them unpeeled in an egg carton in the refrigerator. Then, when

you want to add an egg to a salad, all you have to do is peel and chop.

5. Anytime roast chicken, turkey, pork, or beef is needed, simply purchase a lean chunk from the deli section of your grocery. When a recipe calls for cooked meat, dice as much as you need *right then*. You save roasting time, and you'll have no bones or fatty sections to cut off or throw away.

6. Kitchen shears are wonderful for cutting up canned tomatoes, peaches, or any whole fruit or vegetable in a can. Just snip "whatever" right in the can, then add it to your recipe. No bowl or countertop to clean, either!

JoAnna M. Lund and the Creation of Healthy Exchanges

For twenty-eight years I was the diet queen of DeWitt, Iowa.
I tried every diet I ever heard of, every one I could afford, and every one that found its way to my small town in eastern Iowa. I was willing to try anything that promised to "melt off the pounds," determined to deprive my body in every possible way in order to become thin at last.

I sent away for expensive "miracle" diet pills. I starved myself on the Cambridge Diet and the Bahama Diet. I gobbled Ayds diet candies, took thyroid pills, fiber pills, prescription and over-the-counter diet pills. I went to endless weight-loss support group meetings—but I managed to turn healthy programs such as Overeaters Anonymous, Weight Watchers, and TOPS into unhealthy diets . . . diets I could never follow for more than a few months.

I was determined to discover something that worked long-term, but each new failure increased my desperation that I'd never find it.

I ate strange concoctions and rubbed on even stranger potions. I tried liquid diets like Slimfast and Metrecal. I agreed to be hypnotized. I tried reflexology and even had an acupuncture device stuck in my ear!

Does my story sound a lot like yours? I'm not surprised. No wonder the weight loss business is a billion-dollar industry!

Every new thing I tried seemed to work—at least at first. And losing that first five or ten pounds would get me so excited, I'd believe that this new miracle diet would, finally, get my weight off for keeps.

Inevitably, though, the initial excitement wore off. The diet's routine and boredom set in, and I quit. I shoved the pills to the back of the medicine chest; pushed the cans of powdered shake mix to the rear of the kitchen cabinets; slid all the program materials out of sight under my bed; and once more I felt like a failure.

Like most dieters, I quickly gained back the weight I'd lost each time, along with a few extra "souvenir" pounds that seemed always to settle around my hips. I'd done the diet-lose-weight-gain-it-all-back "yo-yo" on the average of once a year. It's no exaggeration to say that over the years I've lost 1,000 pounds—and gained back 1,150 pounds.

Finally, at the age of forty-six I weighed more than I'd ever imagined possible. I'd stopped believing that any diet could work for me. I drowned my sorrows in sacks of cake donuts, and wondered if I'd live long enough to watch my grandchildren grow up.

Something had to change.

I had to change.

Finally, I did.

I'm just over fifty now—and I'm 130 pounds less than my all-time high of close to 300 pounds. I've kept the weight off for more than six years. I'd like to lose another ten pounds, but I'm not obsessed about it. If it takes me the rest of my life to accomplish it, that's okay.

What I *do* care about is never saying hello again to any of those unwanted pounds I said good-bye to!

How did I jump off the roller coaster I was on? For one thing, I finally stopped looking to food to solve my emotional problems. But what really shook me up—and got me started on the path that changed my life—was Operation Desert Storm in early 1991. I sent three children off to the Persian Gulf War—my son-in-law Matt, a medic in Special Forces; my daughter Becky, a full-time college student and member of a medical unit in the Army Reserve; and my son James, a member of the Inactive Army Reserve reactivated as a chemicals expert.

Somehow, knowing that my children were putting their lives on the line got me thinking about my own mortality—and I knew in my heart the last thing they needed while they were overseas was to get a letter from home saying that their mother was ill because of a food-related problem.

The day I drove the third child to the airport to leave for Saudi Arabia, something happened to me that would change my life for the better—and forever. I stopped praying my constant prayer as a professional dieter, which was simply, "Please, God, let me lose ten pounds by Friday." Instead, I began praying, "God, please help me not be a burden to my kids and my family."

I quit praying for what I wanted, and started praying for what I needed—and in the process my prayers were answered. I couldn't keep the kids safe—that was out of my hands—but I could try to get healthier to better handle the stress of it. It was the least I could do on the homefront.

That quiet prayer was the beginning of the new JoAnna Lund. My initial goal was not to lose weight or create healthy recipes. I only wanted to become healthier for my kids, my husband, and myself.

Each of my children returned safely from the Persian Gulf War. But something didn't come back—the 130 extra pounds I'd been lugging around for far too long. I'd finally accepted the truth after all those agonizing years of suffering through on-again, off-again dieting.

There are no "magic" cures in life.

No "magic" potion, pill, or diet will make unwanted pounds disappear.

I found something better than magic, if you can believe it. When I turned my weight and health dilemma over to God for guidance, a new JoAnna Lund and Healthy Exchanges were born.

I discovered a new way to live my life—and uncovered an unexpected talent for creating easy "common folk" healthy recipes and sharing my commonsense approach to healthy living. I learned that I could motivate others to change their lives and adopt a positive outlook. I began publishing cookbooks and a monthly food newsletter, and speaking to groups all over the country.

I like to say, *"When life handed me a lemon, not only did I make healthy, tasty lemonade, I wrote the recipe down!"*

What I finally found was not a quick fix or a short-term diet, but a great way to live well for a lifetime.

I want to share it with you.

Healthy Exchanges®

Weight Loss

Choices™/Exchanges

If you've ever been on one of the national weight-loss programs like Weight Watchers or Diet Center, you've already been introduced to the concept of measured portions of different food groups that make up your daily food plan. If you are not familiar with such a system of weight-loss choices or exchanges, here's a brief explanation. (If you want or need more detailed information, you can write to the American Dietetic Association or the American Diabetes Association for comprehensive explanations.)

The idea of food exchanges is to divide foods into basic food groups. The foods in each group are measured in servings that have comparable values. These groups include Proteins/Meats, Breads/Starches, Vegetables, Fats, Fruits, Skim Milk, Free Foods, and Optional Calories.

Each choice or exchange included in a particular group has about the same number of calories and a similar carbohydrate, protein, and fat content as the other foods in that group. Because any food on a particular list can be "exchanged" for any other food in that group, it makes sense to call the food groups *exchanges* or *choices*.

I like to think we are also "exchanging" bad habits and food choices for good ones!

By using Weight Loss Choices™ or exchanges you can choose from a variety of foods without having to calculate the nutrient value of each one. This makes it easier to include a wide variety of foods in your daily menus and gives you the opportunity to tailor your choices to your unique appetite.

If you want to lose weight, you should consult your physician or other weight-control expert regarding the number of servings that would be best for you from each food group. Since men generally require more calories than women, and since the requirements for growing children and teenagers differ from those of adults, the right number of exchanges for any one person is a personal decision.

I have included a suggested plan of weight-loss choices in the pages following the exchange lists. It's a program I used to lose 130 pounds, and it's the one I still follow today.

(If you are a diabetic or have been diagnosed with heart problems, it is best to meet with your physician before using this or any other food program or recipe collection.)

Food Group Weight Loss Choices/Exchanges

Not all food group exchanges are alike. The ones that follow are for anyone who's interested in weight loss or maintenance. If you are a diabetic, you should check with your health-care provider or dietitian to get the information you need to help you plan your diet. Diabetic exchanges are calculated by the American Diabetic Association, and information about them is provided in *The Diabetic's Healthy Exchange Cookbook* (Perigee Books).

Every Healthy Exchanges recipe provides calculations in three ways:

- Weight Loss Choices/Exchanges

- Calories, Fat, Protein, Carbohydrates, and Fiber Grams, and Sodium in milligrams

- Diabetic Exchanges calculated for me by a Registered Dietitian

Healthy Exchanges recipes can help you eat well and recover your health, whatever your health concerns may be. Please take a few minutes to review the exchange lists and the suggestions that follow on how to count them. You have lots of great eating in store for you!

Proteins

Meat, poultry, seafood, eggs, cheese, and legumes.
One exchange of Protein is approximately 60 calories. Examples of one Protein choice or exchange:

1 ounce cooked weight of lean meat, poultry, or seafood
2 ounces white fish
1½ ounces 97% fat-free ham
1 egg (limit to no more than 4 per week)
¼ cup egg substitute
3 egg whites
¾ ounce reduced-fat cheese
½ cup fat-free cottage cheese
2 ounces cooked or ¾ ounces uncooked dry beans
1 tablespoon peanut butter (also count 1 fat exchange)

Breads

Breads, crackers, cereals, grains, and starchy vegetables. One exchange of Bread is approximately 80 calories. Examples of one Bread choice/exchange:

1 slice bread or 2 slices reduced-calorie bread (40 calories or less)
1 roll, any type (1 ounce)
½ cup cooked pasta or ¾ ounce uncooked (scant ½ cup)
½ cup cooked rice or 1 ounce uncooked (⅓ cup)
3 tablespoons flour
¾ ounce cold cereal
½ cup cooked hot cereal or ¾ ounce uncooked (2 tablespoons)
½ cup corn (kernels or cream style) or peas
4 ounces white potato, cooked, or 5 ounces uncooked
3 ounces sweet potato, cooked, or 4 ounces uncooked
3 cups air-popped popcorn
7 fat-free crackers (¾ ounce)
3 (2½-inch squares) graham crackers
2 (¾-ounce) rice cakes or 6 mini
1 tortilla, any type (6-inch diameter)

Fruits

All fruits and fruit juices. One exchange of Fruit is approximately 60 calories. Examples of one Fruit choice or exchange:

1 small apple or ½ cup slices
1 small orange
½ medium banana
¾ cup berries (except strawberries and cranberries)
1 cup strawberries or cranberries
½ cup canned fruit, packed in fruit juice or rinsed well
2 tablespoons raisins
1 tablespoon spreadable fruit spread
½ cup apple juice (4 fluid ounces)
½ cup orange juice (4 fluid ounces)
½ cup applesauce

Skim Milk

Milk, buttermilk, and yogurt. One exchange of Skim Milk is approximately 90 calories. Examples of one Skim Milk choice or exchange:

1 cup skim milk
½ cup evaporated skim milk
1 cup low-fat buttermilk
¾ cup plain fat-free yogurt
⅓ cup nonfat dry milk powder

Vegetables

All fresh, canned, or frozen vegetables other than the starchy vegetables. One exchange of Vegetables is approximately 30 calories. Examples of one Vegetable choice or exchange:

½ cup vegetable
¼ cup tomato sauce
1 medium fresh tomato
½ cup vegetable juice

Fats

Margarine, mayonnaise, vegetable oils, salad dressings, olives, and nuts. One exchange of fat is approximately 40 calories. Examples of one Fat choice or exchange:

> 1 teaspoon margarine or 2 teaspoons reduced-calorie margarine
> 1 teaspoon butter
> 1 teaspoon vegetable oil
> 1 teaspoon mayonnaise or 2 teaspoons reduced-calorie mayonnaise
> 1 teaspoon peanut butter
> 1 ounce olives
> ¼ ounce pecans or walnuts

Free Foods

Foods that do not provide nutritional value but are used to enhance the taste of foods are included in the Free Foods group. Examples of these are spices, herbs, extracts, vinegar, lemon juice, mustard, Worcestershire sauce, and soy sauce. Cooking sprays and artificial sweeteners used in moderation are also included in this group. However, you'll see that I include the caloric value of artificial sweeteners in the Optional Calories of the recipes.

You may occasionally see a recipe that lists "free food" as part of the portion. According to the published exchange lists, a free food contains fewer than 20 calories per serving. Two or three servings per day of free foods/drinks are usually allowed in a meal plan.

Optional Calories

Foods that do not fit into any other group but are used in moderation in recipes are included in Optional Calories. Foods that are counted in this way include sugar-free gelatin and puddings, fat-free mayonnaise and dressings, reduced-calorie whipped toppings, reduced-calorie syrups and jams, chocolate chips, coconut, and canned broth.

Sliders™

These are 80 Optional Calorie increments that do not fit into any particular category. You can choose which food groups to *slide* them into. It is wise to limit this selection to approximately three per day to ensure the best possible nutrition for your body while still enjoying an occasional treat.

Sliders may be used in either of the following ways:

1. If you have consumed all your Protein, Bread, Fruit, or Skim Milk Weight Loss Choices for the day, and you want to eat additional foods from those food groups, you simply use a Slider. It's what I call "healthy horse trading." Remember that Sliders may not be traded for choices in the Vegetables or Fats food groups.

2. Sliders may also be deducted from your Optional Calories (OC) for the day or week. ¼ Sl equals 20 OC; ½ Sl equals 40 OC; ¾ Sl equals 60 OC; and 1 Sl equals 80 OC. This way, you can choose the food group to *slide* into.

Healthy Exchanges Weight Loss Choices

Here's my suggested program of Weight Loss Choices, based on an average daily total of 1,400–1,600 calories per day. *If you require more or fewer calories, please revise this plan to your individual needs.*

Each day, women should plan to eat:

2 Skim Milk servings, 90 calories each
2 Fat servings, 40 calories each
3 Fruit servings, 60 calories each
4 Vegetable servings or more, 30 calories each
5 Protein servings, 60 calories each
5 Bread servings, 80 calories each

Men should add to this basic program: 2 Fat servings (for a total of 4), 1 Protein serving (for a total of 6), and 2 Bread servings (for a total of 7).

Young people should follow the program for Men but add 1 Skim Milk serving for a total of 3 servings.

You may also choose to add up to 100 Optional Calories per day, and up to 28 Sliders per week at 80 calories each. If you choose to include more Sliders in your daily or weekly totals, deduct those 80 calories from your Optional Calorie "bank."

A word about **Sliders**. These are to be counted toward your totals after you have used your allotment of choices of Skim Milk, Protein, Bread, and Fruit for the day. By "sliding" an additional choice into one of these groups, you can meet your individual needs for that day. Sliders are especially helpful when traveling, stressed out, eating out, or for special events. I often use mine so I can enjoy my favorite Healthy Exchanges desserts. Vegetables are not to be counted as Sliders. Enjoy as many Vegetable choices as you need to feel satisfied. Because we want to limit our fat intake to moderate amounts, additional Fat choices should not be counted as Sliders. If you choose to include more fat on an *occasional* basis, count the extra choices as Optional Calories.

Keep a daily food diary of your Weight Loss Choices, checking off what you eat as you go. If, at the end of the day, your required selections are not 100 percent accounted for, but you have done the best you could, go to bed with a clear conscience. There will be days when you have ¼ Fruit or ½ Bread left over. What are you going to do—eat two slices of an orange or half a slice of bread and throw the rest out? I always say that "nothing in life comes out exact." Just do the best you can . . . *the best you can.*

Try to drink at least eight glasses of water a day. Water truly is the "nectar" of good health.

As a little added insurance, I take a multivitamin each day. It's not essential, but if my day's worth of well-planned meals "bites the dust" when unexpected events intrude on my regular routine, my body still gets its vital nutrients.

The calories listed in each group of choices are averages. Some choices within each group may be higher or lower, so it's important to select a variety of different foods instead of eating the same three or four all the time.

Use your Optional Calories! They are what I call "life's little extras." They make all the difference in how you enjoy your food and appreciate the variety available to you. Yes, we can get by without them, but do you really want to? Keep in mind that you should be using all your daily Weight Loss Choices first to ensure you are getting the basics of good nutrition. But I guarantee that Optional Calories will keep you from feeling deprived—and help you reach your weight-loss goals.

Sodium, Fat, Cholesterol, and Processed Foods

A re Healthy Exchanges Ingredients Really Healthy?
When I first created Healthy Exchanges, many people asked about sodium, about whether it was necessary to calculate the percentage of fat, saturated fat, and cholesterol in a healthy diet, and about my use of processed foods in many recipes. I researched these questions as I was developing my program, so you can feel confident about using the recipes and food plan.

Sodium

Most people consume more sodium than their bodies need. The American Heart Association and the American Diabetes Association recommend limiting daily sodium intake to no more than 3,000 mg. per day. If your doctor suggests you limit your sodium even more, then *you really must read labels.*

Sodium is an essential nutrient and should not be completely eliminated. It helps to regulate blood volume and is needed for normal daily muscle and nerve functions. Most of us, however, have no trouble getting "all we need" and then some.

As with everything else, moderation is my approach. I rarely ever have salt in my list as an added ingredient. But if you're especially sodium sensitive, make the right choices for you—and save high-sodium foods such as sauerkraut for an occasional treat.

I use lots of spices to enhance flavors, so you won't notice the absence of salt. In the few cases where it is used, it's vital for the success of the recipe, so please don't omit it.

When I do use an ingredient high in sodium, I try to compensate by using low-sodium products in the remainder of the recipe. Many fat-free products are a little higher in sodium to make up for any flavor that disappeared along with the fat. But when I take advantage of these fat-free, higher-sodium products, I stretch that ingredient within the recipe, lowering the amount of sodium per serving. A good example is my use of fat-free canned soups. While the suggested number of servings per can is two, I make sure my final creation serves at least four and sometimes six. So the soup's sodium has been "watered down" from one-third to one-half of the original amount.

Even if you don't have to watch your sodium intake for medical reasons, using moderation is another "healthy exchange" to make on your own journey to good health.

Fat Percentages

We've been told that 30 percent is the magic number—that we should limit fat intake to 30 percent or less of our total calories. It's good advice, and I try to have a weekly average of 15 to 25 percent myself. I believe any less than 15 percent is really just another restrictive diet that won't last. And more than 25 percent on a regular basis is too much of a good thing.

When I started listing fat grams along with calories in my recipes, I was tempted to include the percentage of calories from fat. After all, in the vast majority of my recipes, that percentage is well below 30 percent. This even includes my pie recipes that allow you a realistic serving instead of many "diet" recipes that tell you a serving is 1/12 of a pie.

Figuring fat grams is easy enough. Each gram of fat equals nine calories. Multiply fat grams by 9 then divide that number by the total calories to get the percentage of calories from fat.

So why don't I do it? After consulting four registered dietitians for advice, I decided to omit this information. They felt that it's too easy for people to become obsessed by that 30 percent figure, which is after all supposed to be a percentage of total calories over the course of a day or a week. We mustn't feel we can't include a healthy ingredient such as pecans or olives in one recipe just because, on its own, it has more than 30 percent of its calories from fat.

An example of this would be a casserole made with 90 percent lean red meat. Most of us benefit from eating red meat in moderation, as it provides iron and niacin in our diets, and it also makes life more enjoyable for us and those who eat with us. If we *only* look at the percentage of calories from fat in a serving of this one dish, which might be as high as 40 to 45 percent, we might choose not to include this recipe in our weekly food plan.

The dietitians suggested that it's important to consider the total picture when making such decisions. As long as your overall food plan keeps fat calories to 30 percent, it's all right to enjoy an occasional dish that is somewhat higher in fat content. Healthy foods I include in **MODERATION** include 90 percent lean red meat, olives, and nuts. I don't eat these foods every day, and you may not either. But occasionally, in a good recipe, they make all the difference in the world between just getting by (deprivation) and truly enjoying your food.

Remember, the goal is eating in a healthy way so you can enjoy and live well the rest of your life.

Saturated Fats and Cholesterol

You'll see that I don't provide calculations for saturated fats or cholesterol amounts in my recipes. It's for the simple and yet not so simple reason that accurate, up-to-date, brand-specific information can be difficult to obtain from food manufacturers, especially since the way in which they produce food keeps changing rapidly. But once more I've consulted with registered dietitians and other professionals and found that because I use only a few products that are high in saturated fat, and use them in such limited quantities, my recipes are suitable for patients concerned about controlling or lowering cholesterol. You'll also find that whenever I do use one of these ingredients *in moderation*, everything else in the recipe, and in the meals my family and I enjoy, is low in fat.

Processed Foods

Some people have asked how "healthy" recipes can so often use "processed foods"—ready-made products like canned soups, prepared piecrusts, frozen potatoes, and frozen whipped topping? Well, I believe that such foods, used properly (that word **moderation** again) as part of a healthy lifestyle, have a place as ingredients in healthy recipes.

I'm not in favor of spraying everything we eat with chemicals, and I don't mean that all our foods should come out of packages. But I do think we should use the best available products to make cooking easier and foods taste better. I take advantage of good low-fat and low-sugar products, and my recipes are created for busy people like me who want to eat well and eat healthy. I don't expect people to visit out-of-the-way health food stores or find time to cook beans from scratch—*because I don't*. There are lots of very good processed foods available in your local grocery store, and they can make it so much easier to enjoy the benefits of healthy eating.

I certainly don't recommend that everything you eat come from a can, box, or jar. In the best of all possible worlds I would start with the basics: rice, poultry, fish, or beef, and raw vegetables— then throw in a can of reduced-sodium/97 percent fat-free soup (a processed food), and end up with an appetizing, easy-to-prepare, healthy meal.

Most of us can't grow fresh food in the backyard, and many people don't even have a nearby farmer's market. But instead of saying, "Well, I can't get to the health food store so why not eat that hot fudge sundae?" you gotta play ball in your private ball field, not in someone else's. I want to help you figure out ways to make living healthy **doable** and **livable** *wherever you live*, or you're not going to stick with it.

I've checked with the American Dietetic Association, the American Diabetes Association, and with many registered dietitians, and

I've been assured that sugar-free and fat-free processed products that use substitutes for sugar and fat are safe when used in the intended way. This means a realistic serving, not one hundred cans of diet soda every day of the year! Even carrots can turn your skin orange if you eat far too many, but does anyone suggest we avoid eating carrots?

Of course, it is your privilege to disagree with me and to use whatever you choose when you prepare your food. I never want to be one of those "opinionated" people who think it's their God-given right to make personal decisions for others and insist that their way is the *only* way.

Besides, new research comes out every day that declares one food bad and another food good. Then a few days later, some new information emerges, saying that the opposite is true. When the facts are sifted from the fiction, the truth is probably somewhere in between. I know I feel confused when what was bad for you last year is good for you now, and vice versa.

Instead of listening to unreasonable sermons by naysayers who are nowhere around when it comes time to make a quick and healthy meal for your family, I've tried to incorporate the best processed foods I can find into my Healthy Exchanges recipes. I get stacks of mail from people who are thrilled to discover they can eat good-tasting food and who proudly use processed foods in the intended way. I think you will agree that my commonsense approach to healthy cooking is the right choice for many. Because these foods are convenient, tasty, and good substitutes for less healthy products, people are willing to use them long-term.

So don't let anyone make you feel ashamed for including these products in your healthy lifestyle. Only you can decide what's best for you and your family's needs. Part of living a healthy lifestyle is making those decisions and *getting on with life*.

JoAnna's Ten Commandments of Successful Cooking

A few minutes spent before you start cooking will save you hours in the kitchen. The best use of your time, energy, and money is not only reading these suggestions for conquering the kitchen but also applying them to your daily cooking.

1. **Read the entire recipe from start to finish** and be sure you understand the process involved. Check that you have all the equipment you will need *before* you begin.

2. **Check the ingredient list** and be sure you have *everything* and in the amounts required. Keep cooking sprays handy—while they're not listed as ingredients, I use them all the time (just a quick squirt!).

3. **Set out *all* the ingredients and equipment needed** to prepare the recipe on the counter near you *before* you start. Remember that old saying, *A stitch in time saves nine*. It applies in the kitchen, too.

4. **Do as much advance preparation as possible** before actually cooking. Chop, cut, grate, or do whatever is needed to prepare the ingredients and have them ready before you start to mix. Turn the oven on at least ten minutes before putting food in to bake, to allow the oven to preheat to the proper temperature.

5. **Use a kitchen timer** to tell you when the cooking or baking time is up. Because stove temperatures vary slightly by manufacturer, you may want to set your timer for five minutes less than the suggested time just to prevent overcooking. Check the progress of your dish at that time, then decide if you need the additional minutes or not.

6. **Measure carefully.** Use glass measures for liquids and metal or plastic cups for dry ingredients. My recipes are based on standard measurements. Unless I tell you it's a scant or full cup, measure the cup level.

7. **For best results, follow the recipe instructions exactly.** Feel free to substitute ingredients that *don't tamper* with the basic chemistry of the recipe, but be sure to leave key ingredients alone. For example, you could substitute sugar-free instant chocolate pudding for sugar-free instant butterscotch pudding, but if you used a six-serving package when a four-serving package was listed in the ingredients, or you used instant when cook-and-serve is required, you won't get the right result.

8. **Clean up as you go.** It is much easier to wash a few items at a time than to face a whole counter of dirty dishes later. The same is true for spills on the counter or floor.

9. **Be careful about doubling or halving a recipe.** Though many recipes can be altered successfully to serve more or fewer people, *many cannot.* This is especially true when it comes to spices and liquids. If you try to double a recipe that calls for one teaspoon of pumpkin-pie spice, for example, and you double the spice, you may end up with a too-spicy taste. I usually suggest increasing spices or liquid by 1½ times when doubling a recipe. If it tastes a little bland to you, you can increase the spice to 1¾ times the original amount the next time you prepare the dish. Remember you can always add more, but you can't take it out after it's been stirred in.

   The same is true with liquid ingredients. If you wanted to triple a recipe like my Barbeque Tuna and Noodles because you were planning to serve a crowd, you might think you should use three times as much of every ingredient. Don't, or you could end up with Tuna Noodle Soup! The original recipe calls for 1¾ cups of chunky tomato sauce, so I'd suggest using 3½ cups of sauce when you triple the recipe (or 2¾ cups if you double it). You'll still have a good-tasting dish that won't run all over the plate.

10. **Write your reactions next to each recipe once you've served it.** Yes, that's right, I'm giving you permission to write in this book. It's yours, after all. Ask yourself: Did everyone like it? Did I have to add another half teaspoon of chili seasoning to please my family, who like to live on the spicier side of the street? You may even want to rate the recipe on a scale of 1★ to 4★, depending on what you thought of it. (Four stars would be the top rating— and I hope you'll feel that way about many of my recipes.) Jotting down your comments while they are fresh in your mind will help you personalize the recipe to your own taste the next time you prepare it.

My Best Healthy Exchanges Tips and Tidbits

Measurements, General Cooking Tips, and Basic Ingredients

The word **moderation** best describes **my use of fats, sugar substitutes**, and **sodium** in these recipes. Wherever possible, I've used cooking spray for sautéing and for browning meats and vegetables. I also use reduced-calorie margarine and no-fat mayonnaise and salad dressings. Lean ground turkey *or* ground beef can be used in the recipes. Just be sure whatever you choose is at least *90 percent lean.*

I've also included **small amounts of sugar and brown sugar substitutes as the sweetening agent** in many of the recipes. I don't drink a hundred cans of soda a day or eat enough artificially sweetened foods in a twenty-four-hour time period to be troubled by sugar substitutes. But if this is a concern of yours and you *do not* need to watch your sugar intake, you can always replace the sugar substitutes with processed sugar and the sugar-free products with regular ones.

I created my recipes knowing they would also be used by hypoglycemics, diabetics, and those concerned about triglycerides. If you choose to use sugar instead, be sure to count the additional calories.

A word of caution when cooking with *sugar substitutes*: Use *saccharin*-based sweeteners when *heating or baking*. In recipes that don't require heat, **Aspartame** (known as NutraSweet) works well in uncooked dishes but leaves an aftertaste in baked products.

I'm often asked why I use an **8-by-8-inch baking dish** in my recipes. It's for portion control. If the recipe says it serves four, just cut down the center, turn the dish, and cut again. Like magic, there's your serving. Also, if this is the only recipe you are preparing requiring an oven, the square dish fits into a tabletop toaster oven easily and energy can be conserved.

To make life even easier, **whenever a recipe calls for ounce measurements** (other than raw meats) I've included the closest cup equivalent. I need to use my scale daily when creating recipes, so I've measured for you at the same time.

Most of the recipes are for **4 to 6 servings**. If you don't have that many to feed, do what I do: freeze individual portions. Then all you have to do is choose something from the freezer and take it to work for lunch or have your evening meals prepared in advance for the week. In this way, I always have something on hand that is both good to eat and good for me.

Unless a recipe includes hard-boiled eggs, cream cheese, mayonnaise, or a raw vegetable or fruit, **the leftovers should freeze well**. (I've marked recipes that freeze well with the symbol of a **snowflake ❄.**) This includes most of the cream pies. Divide any recipe up into individual servings and freeze for your own "TV" dinners.

Another good idea is **cutting leftover pie into individual pieces and freezing each one separately** in a small Ziploc freezer bag. Then the next time you want to thaw a piece of pie for yourself, you don't have to thaw the whole pie. It's great this way for brown-bag lunches, too. Just pull a piece out of the freezer on your way to work and by lunchtime you will have a wonderful dessert waiting for you.

Unless I specify **"covered" for simmering or baking**, prepare my recipes **uncovered**. Occasionally you will read a recipe that asks you to cover a dish for a time, then to uncover, so read the directions carefully to avoid confusion—and to get the best results.

Low-fat cooking spray is another blessing in a Healthy Exchanges kitchen. It's currently available in three flavors . . .

- OLIVE OIL–FLAVORED when cooking Mexican, Italian, or Greek dishes

- BUTTER FLAVORED when the hint of butter is desired

- REGULAR for everything else

A quick spray of the butter-flavored kind makes air-popped popcorn a low-fat taste treat, or try it as a butter substitute on steaming hot corn on the cob. One light spray of the skillet when browning meat will convince you that you're using "old fashioned fat," and a quick coating of the casserole dish before you add the ingredients will make serving easier and cleanup quicker.

I use reduced-sodium **canned chicken broth** in place of dry bouillon to lower the sodium content. The intended flavor is still present in the prepared dish. As a reduced-sodium beef broth is not currently available (at least not in DeWitt, Iowa), I use the canned regular beef broth. The sodium content is still lower than regular dry bouillon.

Whenever **cooked rice or pasta** is an ingredient, follow the package directions, but eliminate the salt and/or margarine called for. This helps lower the sodium and fat content. It tastes just fine; trust me on this.

Here's another tip: When **cooking rice or noodles**, why not cook extra "for the pot"? After you use what you need, store leftover rice in a covered container (where it will keep for a couple of days). With noodles like spaghetti or macaroni, first rinse and drain as usual, then measure out what you need. Put the leftovers, covered with water, in a bowl, then store in the refrigerator, covered, until they're needed. Then, measure out what you need, rinse and drain them, and they're ready to go.

Does your **pita bread** often tear before you can make a sandwich? Here's my tip to make it open easily: cut the bread in half, put the halves in the microwave for about 15 seconds, and they will open up by themselves. Voilà!

When **chunky salsa** is listed as an ingredient, I leave the degree of "heat" up to your personal taste. In our house, I'm considered a wimp. I go for the "mild" while Cliff prefers "extra-hot." How do we compromise? I prepare the recipe with mild salsa because he can always add a spoonful or two of the hotter version to his serving, but I can't enjoy the dish if it's too spicy for me.

Proteins

I use eggs in moderation. I enjoy the real thing on an average of three to four times a week. So, my recipes are calculated on using whole eggs. However, if you choose to use egg substitutes in place of the egg, the finished product will turn out just fine and the fat grams per serving will be even lower than those listed.

If you like the look, taste, and feel of **hard-boiled eggs** in salads but haven't been using them because of the cholesterol in the yolk, I have a couple of alternatives for you. (1) Pour an 8-ounce carton of egg substitute into a medium skillet sprayed with cooking spray. Cover skillet tightly and cook over low heat until substitute is just set, about 10 minutes. Remove from heat and let set, still covered, for 10 minutes more. Uncover and cool completely. Chop set mixture. This will make about 1 cup of chopped egg. (2) Even easier is to hard-boil "real eggs," toss the yolk away, and chop the white. Either way, you don't deprive yourself of the pleasure of egg in your salad.

In most recipes calling for **egg substitutes**, you can use 2 egg whites in place of the equivalent of 1 egg substitute. Just break the eggs open and toss the yolks away. I can hear some of you already saying, "But that's wasteful!" Well, take a look at the price on the egg substitute package (which usually has the equivalent of 4 eggs in it), then look at the price of a dozen eggs, from which you'd get the equivalent of 6 egg substitutes. Now, what's wasteful about that?

Whenever I include **cooked chicken** in a recipe, I use roasted white meat without skin. Whenever I include **roast beef or pork** in a recipe, I use the loin cuts because they are much leaner. However, most of the time, I do my roasting of all these meats at the local deli. I just ask for a chunk of their lean roasted meat, 6 or 8 ounces, and ask them to slice it. When I get home, I cube or dice the meat and am ready to use it in my recipe. The reason I do this is threefold. (1) I'm getting just the amount I need without leftovers. (2) I don't have the expense of heating the oven. (3) I'm not throwing away the bone, gristle, and fat I'd be cutting away from the meat. Overall, it is probably cheaper to "roast" it the way I do.

Did you know that you can make an acceptable meat loaf without using egg for the binding? Just replace every egg with ¼ cup of liquid. You could use beef broth, tomato sauce, even applesauce, to name just a few alternatives. For a meat loaf to serve six, I always use one pound of extra-lean ground beef or turkey, six tablespoons of dried fine bread crumbs, and ¼ cup of the liquid, plus anything else healthy that strikes my fancy at the time. I mix well and place the mixture in an 8-by-8-inch baking dish or 9-by-5-inch loaf pan sprayed with cooking spray. Bake uncovered at 350 degrees for 35 to 50 minutes (depending on the added ingredients). You will never miss the egg.

Anytime you are **browning ground meat** for a casserole and want to get rid of almost all of the excess fat, just place the uncooked meat loosely in a plastic colander. Set the colander in a glass pie plate. Place in a microwave and cook on High for three to six minutes (depending on the amount being browned), stirring often. Use as you would for any casserole. You can also chop up onions and brown them with the meat if you want to.

Milk and Yogurt

Take it from me—nonfat dry milk powder is great! I *do not* use it for drinking, but I *do* use it for cooking. Three good reasons why:

1. It is very **inexpensive**.

2. It does not sour because you use it only as needed. Store the box in your refrigerator or freezer and it will keep almost forever.

3. You can easily **add extra calcium** to just about any recipe without added liquid.

I consider nonfat dry milk powder one of Mother Nature's modern-day miracles of convenience. But do purchase a good national name brand (I like Carnation), and keep it fresh by proper storage.

In many of my pies and puddings, I use nonfat dry milk powder and water instead of skim milk. Usually I call for ⅔ cup nonfat dry milk powder and 1¼ to 1½ cups water or liquid. This way I can get the nutrients of two cups of milk, but much less liquid, and the end result is much creamier. Also, the recipe sets up more quickly, usually in 5 minutes or less. So if someone knocks at your door unexpectedly at mealtime, you can quickly throw a pie together and enjoy it minutes later.

You can make your own "**sour cream**" by combining ¾ cup plain fat-free yogurt with ⅓ cup nonfat dry milk powder. What you did by doing this is fourfold: (1) The dry milk stabilizes the yogurt and keeps the whey from separating. (2) The dry milk slightly helps to cut the tartness of the yogurt. (3) It's still virtually fat-free. (4) The calcium has been increased by 100 percent. Isn't it great how we can make that distant relative of sour cream a first kissin' cousin by adding the nonfat dry milk powder? Or, if you place 1 cup of plain fat-free yogurt in a sieve lined with a coffee filter, and place the sieve over a small bowl and refrigerate for about 6 hours, you will end up with a very good alternative for sour cream. To **stabilize yogurt** when cooking or baking with it, just add 1 teaspoon corn-starch to every ¾ cup yogurt.

If a recipe calls for **evaporated skim milk** and you don't have any in the cupboard, make your own. For every ½ cup evaporated skim milk needed, combine ⅓ cup nonfat dry milk powder and ½ cup water. Use as you would evaporated skim milk.

You can also make your own **sugar-free and fat-free sweetened condensed milk** at home. Combine 1⅓ cups nonfat dry milk powder and ½ cup cold water in a 2-cup glass measure. Cover and microwave on High until mixture is hot but *not* boiling. Stir in ½ cup Sprinkle Sweet or Sugar Twin. Cover and refrigerate at least 4 hours. This mixture will keep for up to two weeks in the refrigerator. Use in just about any recipe that calls for sweetened condensed milk.

For any recipe that calls for **buttermilk**, you might want to try Jo's Buttermilk: Blend one cup of water and ⅔ cup dry milk powder (the nutrients of two cups of skim milk). It'll be thicker than this mixed-up milk usually is, because it's doubled. Add 1 teaspoon white vinegar and stir, then let it sit for at least ten minutes.

One of my subscribers was looking for a way to further restrict salt intake and needed a substitute for **cream of mushroom soup**. For many of my recipes, I use Healthy Request Cream of Mushroom soup, as it is a reduced-sodium product. The label suggests two servings per can, but I usually incorporate the soup into a recipe serving at least four. By doing this, I've reduced the sodium in the soup by half again.

But if you must restrict your sodium even more, try making my Healthy Exchanges **Creamy Mushroom Sauce**. Place 1½ cups evaporated skim milk and 3 tablespoons flour in a covered jar. Shake well and pour mixture into a medium saucepan sprayed with butter-flavored cooking spray. Add ½ cup canned sliced mushrooms, rinsed and drained. Cook over medium heat, stirring often, until mixture thickens. Add any seasonings of your choice. You can use this sauce in any recipe that calls for one 10¾-ounce can of cream of mushroom soup.

Why did I choose these proportions and ingredients?

- 1½ cups of evaporated skim milk is the amount in one can.

- It's equal to three milk choices or exchanges.

- It's the perfect amount of liquid and flour for a medium cream sauce.

- Three tablespoons of flour are equal to one Bread/Starch choice or exchange.

- Any leftovers will reheat beautifully with a flour-based sauce, but not with a cornstarch base.

- The mushrooms are one vegetable choice or exchange.

- This sauce is virtually fat free, sugar free, and sodium free.

Fruits and Vegetables

If you want to enjoy a **"fruit shake"** with some pizazz, just combine soda water and unsweetened fruit juice in a blender. Add crushed ice. Blend on High until thick. Refreshment without guilt.

You'll see that many recipes use ordinary **canned vegetables**. They're much cheaper than reduced-sodium versions, and once you rinse and drain them, the sodium is reduced anyway. I believe in saving money wherever possible so we can afford the best in fat-free and sugar-free products as they come onto the market.

All three kinds of **vegetables—fresh, frozen, and canned—** have their place in a healthy diet. My husband, Cliff, hates the taste of frozen or fresh green beans, thinks the texture is all wrong, so I use canned green beans instead. In this case, canned vegetables have their proper place when I'm feeding my husband. If someone in your family has a similar concern, it's important to respond to it so everyone can be happy and enjoy the meal.

When I use **fruits or vegetables** like apples, cucumbers, and zucchini, I wash them really well and **leave their skin on**. It provides added color, fiber, and attractiveness to any dish. And, because I use processed flour in my cooking, I like to increase the fiber in my diet by eating my fruits and vegetables in their closest-to-natural state.

To help keep **fresh fruits and veggies fresh**, just give them a quick "shower" with lemon juice. The easiest way to do this is to pour purchased lemon juice into a kitchen spray bottle and store in the refrigerator. Then, every time you use fresh fruits or vegetables in a salad or dessert, simply give them a quick spray with your "lemon spritzer." You just might be amazed by how well this little trick keeps your produce from turning brown so fast.

The next time you warm canned vegetables such as carrots or green beans, drain and heat the vegetables in ¼ cup beef or chicken broth. It gives a nice variation to an old standby. Here's how a simple **white sauce** for vegetables and casseroles can be made without using added fat by spraying a medium saucepan with butter-flavored cooking spray: Place 1½ cups evaporated skim milk and 3 tablespoons flour in a covered jar. Shake well. Pour into sprayed saucepan and cook over medium heat until thick, stirring constantly. Add salt and pepper to taste. You can also add ½ cup canned drained mushrooms and/or 3 ounces (¾ cup) shredded reduced-fat cheese. Continue cooking until cheese melts.

Zip up canned or frozen green beans with **chunky salsa**: ½ cup to 2 cups beans. Heat thoroughly. Chunky salsa also makes a wonderful dressing on lettuce salads. It only counts as a vegetable, so enjoy.

Another wonderful **South of the Border** dressing can be stirred up by using ½ cup of chunky salsa and ¼ cup of fat-free Ranch dressing. Cover and store in your refrigerator. Use as a dressing for salads or as a topping for baked potatoes.

For **gravy** with all the "old time" flavor but without the extra fat, try this almost effortless way to prepare it. (It's almost as easy as opening up a store-bought jar.) Pour the juice off your roasted meat, then set the roast aside to "rest" for about 20 minutes. Place the juice in an uncovered cake pan or other large flat pan (we want the large air surface to speed up the cooling process) and put it in the freezer until the fat congeals on top and you can skim it off. Or, if you prefer, use a skimming pitcher purchased at your kitchen gadget store. Either way, measure about 1½ cups skimmed broth and pour into a medium saucepan. Cook over medium heat until heated through, about five minutes. In a covered jar, combine ½ cup water or cooled potato broth with 3 tablespoons flour. Shake well. Pour flour mixture into warmed juice. Combine well using a wire whisk. Continue cooking until gravy thickens, about 5 minutes. Season with salt and pepper to taste.

Why did I use flour instead of cornstarch? Because any leftovers will reheat nicely with the flour base and would not with a cornstarch base. Also, 3 tablespoons of flour works out to 1 Bread/Starch exchange. This virtually fat-free gravy makes about 2 cups, so you could spoon about ½ cup gravy on your low-fat mashed potatoes and only have to count your gravy as ¼ Bread/Starch exchange.

Desserts

Thaw **lite whipped topping** in the refrigerator overnight. Never try to force the thawing by stirring or using a microwave to soften. Stirring it will remove the air from the topping that gives it the lightness and texture we want, and there's not enough fat in it to survive being heated.

How can I **frost an entire pie with just ½ cup of whipped**

topping? First, don't use an inexpensive brand. I use Cool Whip Lite or La Creme lite. Make sure the topping is fully thawed. Always spread from the center to the sides using a rubber spatula. This way, ½ cup topping will literally cover an entire pie. Remember, the operative word is **frost**, not pile the entire container on top of the pie!

Here's a way to **extend the flavor (and oils) of purchased whipped topping:** Blend together ¾ cup plain nonfat yogurt and ⅓ cup nonfat dry milk powder. Add sugar substitute to equal 2 tablespoons sugar, 1 cup Cool Whip Lite and 1 teaspoon of the flavoring of your choice (vanilla, coconut, or almond are all good choices). Gently mix and use as you would whipped topping. The texture is almost a cross between marshmallow cream and whipped cream. This is enough to mound high on a pie.

For a different taste when preparing sugar-free instant pudding mixes, use ¾ cup plain fat-free yogurt for one of the required cups of milk. Blend as usual. It will be *thicker and creamier*. And, no it doesn't taste like yogurt. Another variation for the sugar-free instant vanilla pudding is to use 1 cup skim milk and 1 cup crushed pineapple juice. Mix as usual.

For a special treat that tastes anything but "diet," try placing **spreadable fruit** in a container and microwave for about 15 seconds. Then pour the melted fruit spread over a serving of nonfat ice cream or frozen yogurt. One tablespoon of spreadable fruit is equal to 1 fruit serving. Some combinations to get you started are apricot over chocolate ice cream, strawberry over strawberry ice cream, or any flavor over vanilla. Another way I use spreadable fruit is to make a delicious **topping for a cheesecake or angel food cake.** I take ½ cup of fruit and ½ cup Cool Whip Lite and blend the two together with a teaspoon of coconut extract.

Here's a really **good topping** for the fall of the year. Place 1½ cups of unsweetened applesauce in a medium saucepan or 4-cup glass measure. Stir in two tablespoons of raisins, 1 teaspoon of apple-pie spice, and two tablespoons of Cary's sugar-free maple syrup. Cook over medium heat on the stove or process on High in the microwave until warm. Then spoon about ½ cup of the warm mixture over pancakes, French toast, or fat-free and sugar-free vanilla ice cream. It's as close as you will get to guilt-free apple pie!

A quick yet tasty way to prepare **strawberries for shortcake** is to place about ¾ cup of sliced strawberries, 2 tablespoons of Diet Mountain Dew, and sugar substitute to equal ¼ cup sugar in a blender container. Process on Blend until the mixture is smooth. Pour the mixture into a bowl. Add 1¼ cups of sliced strawberries and mix well. Cover and refrigerate until ready to serve with short-cakes.

The next time you are making treats for the family, try using **unsweetened applesauce** for some or all of the required oil in the recipe. For instance, if the recipe calls for ½ cup of cooking oil, use up to the ½ cup in applesauce. It works and most people will not even notice the difference. It's great in purchased cake mixes, but so far I haven't been able to figure out a way to deep-fat fry with it!

Another trick I often use is to include tiny amounts of "real people" food, such as coconut, but extend the flavor by using extracts. Try it—you will be surprised by how little of the real thing you can use and still feel you are not being deprived.

If you are preparing a pie filling that has ample moisture, just line **graham crackers** in the bottom of a 9-by-9-inch cake pan. Pour the filling over the top of the crackers. Cover and refrigerate until the moisture has had enough time to soften the crackers. Overnight is best. This eliminates the added **fats and sugars of a piecrust**.

When **stirring fat-free cream cheese to soften it**, use only a sturdy spoon, never an electric mixer. The speed of a mixer can cause the cream cheese to lose its texture and become watery.

Did you know you can make your own **fruit-flavored yogurt?** Mix 1 tablespoon of any flavor of spreadable fruit spread with ¾ cup of plain yogurt. It's every bit as tasty and much cheaper. You can also make your own **lemon yogurt** by combining 3 cups of plain fat-free yogurt with 1 tub of Crystal Light lemonade powder. Mix well, cover, and store in the refrigerator. I think you will be pleasantly surprised by the ease, cost, and flavor of this "made from scratch" calcium-rich treat. P.S.: You can make any flavor you like by using any of the Crystal Light mixes—Cranberry? Iced tea? You decide.

Sugar-free puddings and gelatins are important to many of my recipes, but if you prefer to avoid sugar substitutes, you could still prepare the recipes with regular puddings or gelatins. The calories would be higher, but you would still be cooking low-fat.

When a recipe calls for **chopped nuts** (and you only have

whole ones), who wants to dirty the food processor just for a couple of tablespoons? You could try to chop them using your cutting board, but be prepared for bits and pieces to fly all over the kitchen. I use "Grandma's food processor." I take the biggest nuts I can find, put them in a small glass bowl, and chop them into chunks just the right size using a metal biscuit cutter.

If you have a **leftover muffin** and are looking for something a little different for breakfast, you can make a **"breakfast sundae."** Crumble the muffin into a cereal bowl. Sprinkle a serving of fresh fruit over it and top with a couple of tablespoons of nonfat plain yogurt sweetened with sugar substitute and your choice of extract. The thought of it just might make you jump out of bed with a smile on your face. (Speaking of muffins, did you know that if you fill the unused muffin wells with water when baking muffins, you help ensure more even baking and protect the muffin pan at the same time?) Another muffin hint: lightly spray the inside of paper baking cups with butter-flavored cooking spray before spooning the muffin batter into them. Then you won't end up with paper clinging to your fresh-baked muffins.

The secret of making **good meringues** without sugar is to use 1 tablespoon of Sprinkle Sweet or Sugar Twin for every egg white, and a small amount of extract. Use ½ to 1 teaspoon for the batch. Almond, vanilla, and coconut are all good choices. Use the same amount of cream of tartar you usually do. Bake the meringue in the same old way. Don't think you can't have meringue pies because you can't eat sugar. You can, if you do it my way. (Remember that egg whites whip up best at room temperature.)

Homemade or Store-Bought?

I've been asked which is better for you, homemade from scratch or purchased foods. My answer is *both*! They each have a place in a healthy lifestyle, and what that place is has everything to do with you.

Take **piecrusts**, for instance. If you love spending your spare time in the kitchen preparing foods, and you're using low-fat, low-sugar, and reasonably low-sodium ingredients, go for it! But if, like so many people, your time is limited and you've learned to read labels, you could be better off using purchased foods.

I know that when I prepare a pie (and I experiment with a couple of pies each week, because this is Cliff's favorite dessert), I use a purchased crust. Why? Mainly because I can't make a good-tasting piecrust that is lower in fat than the brands I use. Also, purchased piecrusts fit my rule of "If it takes longer to cook it than eat it, forget it!"

I've checked the nutrient information for the purchased piecrust against recipes for traditional and "diet" piecrusts, using my computer software program. The purchased crust calculated lower in both fat and calories! I have tried some low-fat and low-sugar recipes, but they just don't spark my taste buds, or were so complicated you needed an engineering degree just to get the crust in the pie plate.

I'm very happy with the purchased piecrusts in my recipes, because the finished product rarely, if ever, has more than 30 percent of total calories coming from fat. I also believe that we have to prepare foods our families and friends will eat with us on a regular basis and not feel deprived, or we've wasted our time, energy, and money.

I could use a purchased "lite" **pie filling**, but instead I make my own. Here I can save both fat and sugar, and still make the filling almost as fast as opening a can. The bottom line: know what you have to spend when it comes to both time and fat/sugar calories, then make the best decision you can for you and your family. And don't go without an occasional piece of pie because you think it isn't *necessary*. A delicious pie prepared in a healthy way is one of the simple pleasures of life. It's a little thing, but it can make all the difference between just getting by with the bare minimum and living a full and healthy lifestyle.

Many people have experimented with my tip about **substituting applesauce and artificial sweetener for butter and sugar**, but what if you aren't satisfied with the result? One woman wrote to me about a recipe for her grandmother's cookies that called for 1 cup of butter and 1½ cups of sugar. Well, any recipe that depends on as much butter and sugar as this one does is generally not a good candidate for "healthy exchanges." The original recipe needed a large quantity of fat to produce the crisp cookies just like the ones Grandma made.

Unsweetened applesauce can be used to substitute for vegetable oil with various degrees of success, but not to replace butter, lard, or margarine. If your recipe calls for ½ cup oil or less, and it's a quick bread, muffin, or bar cookie, replacing the oil with applesauce should work. If the recipe calls for more than ½ cup oil, then experiment with half oil, half applesauce. You've still made the recipe healthier, even if you haven't removed all the oil from it.

Another rule for healthy substitution: up to ½ cup of sugar or less can be replaced by *an artificial sweetener* (like Sugar Twin or Sprinkle Sweet) *that can withstand the heat of baking*. If it requires more than ½ cup sugar, cut the amount needed by 75 percent and use ½ cup sugar substitute and sugar for the rest. Other options: reduce the butter and sugar by 25 percent and see if the finished product still satisfies you in taste and appearance. Or, make the cookies just the way Grandma did, realizing they are part of your family's holiday tradition. Enjoy a moderate serving of a couple of cookies once or twice during the season, and just forget about them the rest of the year.

I'm sure you'll add to this list of cooking tips as you begin preparing Healthy Exchanges recipes and discover how easy it can be to adapt your own favorite recipes using these ideas and your own common sense.

A Peek Into My Pantry and My Favorite Brands

Everyone asks me what foods I keep on hand and what brands I use. There are lots of good products on the grocery shelves today—many more than we dreamed about even a year or two ago. And I can't wait to see what's out there twelve months from now. The following are my staples and, where appropriate, my favorites *at this time*. I feel these products are healthier, tastier, easy to get—and deliver the most flavor for the least amount of fat, sugar, or calories. If you find others you like as well *or better*, please use them. This is only a guide to make your grocery shopping and cooking easier.

Fat-free plain yogurt (*Yoplait*)
Nonfat dry skim milk powder (*Carnation*)
Evaporated skim milk (*Carnation*)
Skim milk
Fat-free cottage cheese
Fat-free cream cheese (*Philadelphia*)
Fat-free mayonnaise (*Kraft*)
Fat-free salad dressings (*Kraft*)
Fat-free sour cream (*Land O Lakes*)
Reduced-calorie margarine (*Weight Watchers, Promise, or Smart Beat*)
Cooking spray:
   Olive oil–flavored and regular (*Pam*)

Butter flavored for sautéing (*Weight Watchers*)
Butter flavored for spritzing *after* cooking (*I Can't Believe It's Not Butter!*)
Vegetable oil (*Puritan Canola Oil*)
Reduced-calorie whipped topping (*Cool Whip Lite*)
Sugar Substitute:
　If no heating is involved (*Equal*)
　If heating is required:
　　white (*Sugar Twin or Sprinkle Sweet*)
　　brown (*Brown Sugar Twin*)
Sugar-free gelatin and pudding mixes (*JELL-O*)
Baking mix (*Bisquick Reduced-Fat*)
Pancake mix (*Aunt Jemima Reduced Calorie*)
Reduced-calorie pancake syrup (*Cary's Sugar Free*)
Parmesan cheese (*Kraft Fat Free or Weight Watchers Fat Free*)
Reduced-fat cheese (*Kraft ⅓ Less Fat and Weight Watchers*)
Shredded frozen potatoes (*Mr. Dell's*)
Spreadable fruit spread (*Smucker's, Welch's or Sorrell Ridge*)
Peanut butter (*Peter Pan Reduced Fat, Jif Reduced Fat, or Skippy Reduced Fat*)
Chicken broth (*Healthy Request*)
Beef broth (*Swanson*)
Tomato sauce (*Hunts—Chunky and Regular*)
Canned soups (*Healthy Request*)
Tomato juice (*Campbell's Reduced Sodium*)
Ketchup (*Heinz Lite Harvest or Healthy Choice*)
Purchased piecrust:
　unbaked (*Pillsbury—from dairy case*)
　graham cracker, butter flavored, or chocolate flavored (*Keebler*)
Pastrami and corned beef (*Carl Buddig Lean*)
Luncheon meats (*Healthy Choice or Oscar Mayer*)
Ham (*Dubuque 97% fat free and reduced sodium or Healthy Choice*)
Frankfurters and Kielbasa sausage (*Healthy Choice*)
Canned white chicken, packed in water (*Swanson*)
Canned tuna, packed in water (*Starkist*)
90-percent-lean ground turkey and beef
Soda crackers (*Nabisco Fat Free*)

Reduced-calorie bread—40 calories per slice or less
Hamburger buns—80 calories each (*Colonial Old Fashion or Less*)
Rice—instant, regular, brown, and wild
Instant potato flakes (*Betty Crocker Potato Buds*)
Noodles, spaghetti, and macaroni
Salsa (*Chi-Chi's Mild*)
Pickle relish—dill, sweet, and hot dog
Mustard—Dijon, prepared, and spicy
Unsweetened apple juice
Unsweetened applesauce
Fruit—fresh, frozen (no sugar added), or canned in juice
Vegetables—fresh, frozen, or canned
Spices—JO's Spices
Lemon and lime juice (in small plastic fruit-shaped bottles found in produce section)
Instant fruit beverage mixes (*Crystal Light*)
Dry dairy beverage mixes (*Nestlé's Quik and Swiss Miss*)
"Ice cream"—*Well's Blue Bunny Health Beat Fat and Sugar Free*

The items on my shopping list are everyday foods found in just about any grocery store in America. But all are as low in fat, sugar, calories, and sodium as I can find—and that still taste good! I can make any recipe in my cookbooks and newsletters as long as I have my cupboards and refrigerator stocked with these items. Whenever I use the last of any one item, I just make sure I pick up another supply the next time I'm at the store.

If your grocer does not stock these items, why not ask if they can be ordered on a trial basis? If the store agrees to do so, be sure to tell your friends to stop by, so that sales are good enough to warrant restocking the new products. Competition for shelf space is fierce, so only products that sell well stay around.

Shopping the Healthy Exchanges Way

Sometimes, as part of a cooking demonstration, I take the group on a field trip to the nearest supermarket. There's no better place to share my discoveries about which healthy products taste best, which are best for you, and which healthy products don't deliver enough taste to include in my recipes.

While I'd certainly enjoy accompanying you to your neighborhood store, we'll have to settle for a field trip *on paper*. I've tasted and tried just about every fat- and sugar-free product on the market, but so many new ones keep coming out all the time, you're going to have to learn to play detective on your own. I've turned label reading into an art, but often the label doesn't tell me everything I need to know.

Sometimes you'll find, as I have, that the product with *no* fat doesn't provide the taste satisfaction you require; other times, a no-fat or low-fat product just doesn't cook up the same way as the original product. And some foods, including even the leanest meats, can't eliminate *all* the fat. That's okay, though—a healthy diet should include anywhere from 15 to 25 percent of total calories from fat on any given day.

Take my word for it—your supermarket is filled with lots of delicious foods that can and should be part of your healthy diet for life. Come, join me as we check it out on the way to the checkout!

First stop, the **salad dressing** aisle. Salad dressing is usually a high-fat food, but there are great alternatives available. Let's look first at the regular Ranch dressing—2 tablespoons have 170 calories and 18 grams of fat—and who can eat just 2 tablespoons? Already, that's about half the fat grams most people should consume in a day. Of course, it's the most flavorful too. Now let's look at the low-fat version. Two tablespoons have 110 calories and 11 grams of fat; they took about half of the fat out, but there's still a lot of sugar there. The fat-free version has 50 calories and zero grams of fat, but they also took most of the flavor out. Here's what you do to get it back: add a tablespoon of fat-free mayonnaise, a few more parsley flakes, and about a half teaspoon of sugar substitute to your two-tablespoon serving. That trick, with the fat-free mayo and sugar substitute, will work with just about any fat-free dressing and give it more of that full-bodied flavor of the high-fat version. Be careful not to add too much sugar substitute—you don't want it to become sickeningly sweet.

I even use Kraft fat-free **mayonnaise** at 10 calories per table-spoon to make scalloped potatoes. The Smart Beat brand is also a good one.

Before I buy anything at the store, I read the label carefully: the total fat plus the saturated fat; I look to see how many calories are in a realistic serving, and I say to myself, would I eat that much—or would I eat more? I look at the sodium and I look at the total carbohydrates. I like to check those ingredients because I'm cooking for diabetics and heart patients, too. And I check the total calories from fat.

Remember that 1 fat gram equals 9 calories, while 1 protein or 1 carbohydrate gram equals 4 calories.

A wonderful new product is I Can't Believe It's Not Butter! spray, with zero calories and zero grams of fat in four squirts. It's great for your air-popped popcorn. As for **light margarine spread**, beware—most of the fat-free brands don't melt on toast, and they don't taste very good either, so I just leave them on the shelf. For the few times I do use a light margarine I tend to buy Smart Beat Ultra, Promise Ultra, or Weight Watchers Light Ultra. The number-one ingredient in them is water. I occasionally use the light mar-garine in cooking, but I don't really put margarine on my toast anymore. I use apple butter or make a spread with fat-free cream cheese mixed with a little spreadable fruit instead.

So far, Pillsbury hasn't released a reduced-fat **crescent roll**, so you'll only get one crescent roll per serving from me. I usually make eight of the rolls serve twelve by using them for a crust. The house brands may be lower in fat but they're usually not as good flavor-wise—and don't quite cover the pan when you use them to make a crust. If you're going to use crescent rolls with lots of other stuff on top, then a house brand might be fine.

The Pillsbury French Loaf makes a wonderful **pizza crust** and fills a giant jelly roll pan. One-fifth of this package "costs" you only 1 gram of fat (and I don't even let you have that much). Once you use this for your pizza crust, you will never go back to anything else instead. I use it to make calzones too.

I only use Philadelphia Fat Free **cream cheese** because it has the best consistency. I've tried other brands, but I wasn't happy with them. Healthy Choice makes lots of great products, but their cream cheese just doesn't work as well with my recipes.

Let's move to the **cheese** aisle. My preferred brand is Kraft ⅓ less fat shredded cheese. I will not use the fat-free versions because *they don't melt*. I would gladly give up sugar and fat, but I will not give up flavor. This is a happy compromise. I use the reduced-fat version. I use less, and I use it where your eyes "eat" it, on top of the recipe. So you walk away satisfied and with a finished product that's very low in fat. If you want to make grilled-cheese sandwiches for your kids, use the Kraft ⅓ less fat cheese slices, and it'll taste exactly like the one they're used to. The fat-free will not.

Some brands have come out with a fat-free **hot dog**, but the ones we've tasted haven't been very good. So far, among the low-fat brands, I think Healthy Choice tastes the best. Did you know that regular hot dogs have as many as 15 grams of fat?

Dubuque's extra-lean reduced-sodium **ham** tastes wonderful, reduces the sodium as well as the fat, and gives you a larger serving. Don't be fooled by products called turkey ham; they may *not* be lower in fat than a very lean pork product. Here's one label as an example: I checked a brand of turkey ham called Genoa. It gives you a 2-ounce serving for 70 calories and 3½ grams of fat. The Dubuque extra-lean ham, made from pork, gives you a 3-ounce serving for 90 calories, but only 2½ grams of fat. *You get more food and less fat.*

The same can be true of packaged **ground turkey**; if you're not buying *fresh* ground turkey, you may be getting a product with turkey skin and a lot of fat ground up in it. Look to be sure the package is labeled with the fat content; if it isn't, run the other way!

Your best bets in **snack foods** are pretzels, which are always low in fat, as well as the chips from the Guiltless Gourmet, which taste especially good with one of my dips.

Frozen dinners can be expensive and high in sodium, but it's smart to have two or three in the freezer as a backup when your best-laid plans go awry and you need to grab something on the run. It's not a good idea to rely on them too much—what if you can't get to the store to get them, or you're short on cash? The sodium can be high in some of them because they often replace the fat with salt, so do read the labels. Also ask yourself if the serving is enough to satisfy you; for many of us, it's not.

Egg substitute is expensive, and probably not necessary unless you're cooking for someone who has to worry about every bit of cholesterol in his or her diet. If you occasionally have a fried egg or an omelet, *use the real egg.* For cooking, you can usually substitute two egg whites for one whole egg. Most of the time it won't make any difference, but check your recipe carefully.

Frozen pizzas aren't particularly healthy, but used occasionally, in moderation, they're okay. Your best bet is to make your own using the Pillsbury French Crust. Take a look at the frozen pizza package of your choice, though, because you may find that plain cheese pizza, which you might think would be the healthiest, might actually have the most fat. Since there's nothing else on there, they have to cover the crust with a heavy layer of high-fat cheese. A veggie pizza generally uses less cheese and more healthy, crunchy vegetables.

Healthy frozen desserts are hard to find except for the Weight Watchers brands. I've always felt that their portions are so small, and for their size still pretty high in fat and sugar. (This is one of the reasons I think I'll be successful marketing my frozen desserts someday.) Keep an eye out for fat-free or very low-fat frozen yogurt or sorbet products. Even Häagen-Dazs, which makes some of the highest-fat-content ice cream, now has a fat-free fruit sorbet pop out that's pretty good. I'm sure there will be more before too long.

You have to be realistic: What are you willing to do, and what are you *not* willing to do? Let's take bread, for example. Some people just have to have the real thing—rye bread with caraway seeds or a whole-wheat version with bits of bran in it.

I prefer to use reduced-calorie **bread** because I like a *real* sandwich. This way, I can have two slices of bread and it counts as only one bread/starch exchange.

Do you love **croutons**? Forget the ones from the grocery store—they're extremely high in fat. Instead, take reduced-calorie bread, toast it, give it a quick spray of I Can't Believe It's Not Butter! spray, and let it dry a bit. Cut the bread in cubes. Then, for an extra-good flavor, put the pieces in a plastic bag with a couple of tablespoons of grated Kraft fat-free Parmesan cheese and shake them up. You might be surprised just how good they are. Here's another product that's really good for croutons—Corn Chex cereal. Sprinkle a few Chex on top of your salad, and I think you'll be pleasantly surprised. I've also found that Rice Chex, crushed up, with parsley flakes and a little bit of Parmesan cheese, makes a great topping for casseroles that you used to put potato chips on.

Salad toppers can make a lot of difference in how content you feel after you've eaten. Some low-fat cheese, some homemade croutons, and even some bacon bits on top of your greens deliver an abundance of tasty satisfaction. I always use the real Hormel **bacon bits** instead of the imitation bacon-flavored bits. I only use a small amount, but you get that real bacon flavor—and less fat, too.

How I Shop

I always keep my kitchen stocked with my basic staples; that way, I can go to the cupboard and create new recipes anytime I'm inspired. I hope you will take the time (and allot the money) to stock your cupboards with items from the staples list, so you can enjoy developing your own healthy versions of family favorites without making extra trips to the market.

I'm always on the lookout for new products sitting on the grocery shelf. When I spot something I haven't seen before, I'll usually grab it, glance at the front, then turn it around and read the label carefully. I call it looking at the promises (the "come-on" on the front of the package) and then at the warranty (the ingredients list and the label on the back).

If it looks as good on the back as it does on the front, I'll say okay and either create a recipe on the spot or take it home for when I do think of something to do with it. Picking up a new product is just about the only time I buy something not on my list.

The items on my shopping list are normal, everyday foods, but as low-fat and low-sugar (*while still tasting good*) as I can find. I can make any recipe in this book as long as these staples are on my shelves. After using these products for a couple of weeks, you will find it becomes routine to have them on hand. And I promise you, I really don't spend any more at the store now than I did a few years ago when I told myself I couldn't afford some of these items. Back then, of course, plenty of unhealthy, high-priced snacks I really didn't need somehow made the magic leap from the grocery shelves into my cart. Who was I kidding?

Yes, you often have to pay a little more for fat-free or low-fat products, including meats. But since I frequently use a half pound of meat to serve four to six people, your cost per serving will be much lower.

Try adding up what you were spending before on chips and cookies, premium brand ice cream and fatty cuts of meat, and you'll soon see that we've *streamlined* your shopping cart—and taken the weight off your pocketbook as well as your hips!

Remember, your good health is *your* business—but it's big business, too. Write to the manufacturers of products you and your family enjoy but feel are just too high in fat, sugar, or sodium to be part of your new healthy lifestyle. Companies are spending millions of dollars to respond to consumers' concerns about food products, and I bet that in the next few years, you'll discover fat-free and low-fat versions of nearly every product piled high on your supermarket shelves!

The Healthy
Exchanges Kitchen

You might be surprised to discover I still don't have a massive test kitchen stocked with every modern appliance and handy gadget ever made. The tiny galley kitchen where I first launched Healthy Exchanges has room for only one person at a time in it, but that never stopped me from feeling the sky's the limit when it comes to seeking out great healthy taste!

Because storage is at such a premium in my kitchen, I don't waste space with equipment I don't really need. Here's a list of what I consider worth having. If you notice serious gaps in your equipment, you can probably find most of what you need at a local discount store or garage sale. If your kitchen is equipped with more sophisticated appliances, don't feel guilty about using them. Enjoy every appliance you can find room for or that you can afford. Just be assured that healthy, quick, and delicious food can be prepared with the "basics."

A Healthy Exchanges
Kitchen Equipment List

Good-quality nonstick skillets (medium, large)
Good-quality saucepans (small, medium, large)

Glass mixing bowls (small, medium, large)
Glass measures (1-cup, 2-cup, 4-cup, 8-cup)
Sharp knives (paring, chef, butcher)
Rubber spatulas
Wire whisks
Measuring spoons
Large mixing spoons
Egg separator
Covered jar
Vegetable parer
Grater
Potato masher
Electric mixer
Electric blender
Electric skillet
Cooking timer
Slow cooker
Air popper for popcorn
4-inch round custard dishes
Glass pie plates
8-by-8-inch glass baking dishes
Cake pans (9-by-9, 9-by-13-inch)
10¾-by-7-by-1½-inch biscuit pan
Cookie sheets (good nonstick ones)
Jelly roll pan
Muffin tins
5-by-9-inch bread pan
Plastic colander
Cutting board
Pie wedge server
Square-shaped server
Can opener (I prefer manual)
Rolling pin
Kitchen scales (unless you *always* use my recipes)
Wire racks for cooling baked goods
Electric toaster oven (to conserve energy for those times
    when only one item is being baked or for a recipe that
    calls for a short baking time)

How to Read a Healthy Exchanges Recipe

The Healthy Exchanges Nutritional Analysis

Before using these recipes, you may wish to consult your physician or health-care provider to be sure they are appropriate for you. The information in this book is not intended to take the place of any medical advice. It reflects my experiences, studies, research, and opinions regarding healthy eating.

Each recipe includes nutritional information calculated in three ways:

> Healthy Exchanges Weight Loss Choices or Exchanges
> Calories, fiber, and fat grams
> Diabetic exchanges

In every Healthy Exchanges recipe, the diabetic exchanges have been calculated by a registered dietitian. All the other calculations were done by computer, using the Food Processor II software. When the ingredient listing gives more than one choice, the first ingredient listed is the one used in the recipe analysis. Due to inevitable variations in the ingredients you choose to use, the nutritional values should be considered approximate.

The annotation "(limited)" following Protein counts in some

recipes indicates that consumption of whole eggs should be limited to four per week.

Please note the following symbols:

☆ This star means read the recipe's directions carefully for special instructions about **division** of ingredients.

❋ This symbol indicates **FREEZES WELL.**

A Few Cooking Terms to Ease the Way

Everyone can learn to cook *The Healthy Exchanges Way*. It's simple, it's quick, and the results are delicious! If you've tended to avoid the kitchen because you find recipe instructions confusing or complicated, I hope I can help you feel more confident. I'm not offering a full cooking course here, just some terms I use often that I know you'll want to understand.

Bake: To cook food in the oven; sometimes called roasting

Beat: To mix very fast with a spoon, wire whisk, or electric mixer

Blend: To mix two or more ingredients together thoroughly so that the mixture is smooth

Boil: To cook in liquid until bubbles form

Brown: To cook at low to medium-low heat until ingredients turn brown

Chop: To cut food into small pieces with a knife, blender, or food processor

Cool: To let stand at room temperature until food is no longer hot to the touch

Combine: To mix ingredients together with a spoon

Dice:	To chop into small, even-sized pieces
Drain:	To pour off liquid; sometimes you will need to reserve the liquid to use in the recipe, so please read carefully
Drizzle:	To sprinkle drops of liquid (for example, chocolate syrup) lightly over top of food
Fold in:	To combine delicate ingredients with other foods by using a gentle, circular motion. Example: adding Cool Whip Lite to an already stirred-up bowl of pudding
Preheat:	To heat your oven to the desired temperature, usually about ten minutes before you put your food in to bake
Sauté:	To cook in a skillet or frying pan until food is soft
Simmer:	To cook in a small amount of liquid over low heat; this lets the flavors blend without too much liquid evaporating
Whisk:	To beat with a wire whisk until mixture is well mixed; don't worry about finesse here, just use some elbow grease!

How to Measure

I try to make it as easy as possible by providing more than one measurement for many ingredients in my recipes—both the weight in ounces and the amount measured by a measuring cup, for example. Just remember:

- You measure **solids** (flour, Cool Whip Lite, yogurt, macaroni, nonfat dry milk powder) in your set of separate measuring cups (¼, ⅓, ½, 1 cup)

- You measure **liquids** (Diet Mountain Dew, water, tomato juice) in the clear glass or plastic measuring cups that measure ounces, cups, and pints. Set the cup on a level surface and pour the liquid into it, or you may get too much.

- You can use your measuring spoon set for liquids or solids. **Note:** Don't pour a liquid like an extract into a measuring spoon held over the bowl and run the risk of overpouring; instead, do it over the sink.

Here are a few handy equivalents:

3 teaspoons	equal	1 tablespoon
4 tablespoons	equal	¼ cup
5⅓ tablespoons	equal	⅓ cup
8 tablespoons	equal	½ cup
10⅔ tablespoons	equal	⅔ cup
12 tablespoons	equal	¾ cup
16 tablespoons	equal	1 cup
2 cups	equal	1 pint
4 cups	equal	1 quart
8 ounces liquid	equal	1 fluid cup

That's it. Now, ready, set, cook!

The Menus

1. Mandarin Orange
   Spinach Salad
   Calico Bean Salad
   Cheesy Rice-Corn Skillet
   Banana Lemon Cream Pie

2. Royal Carrot and Celery
   Salad
   Home-Style Green Beans
   Mexican Onion and
   Spaghetti Skillet
   Chocolate Peppermint Pie

3. Cabbage Patch Slaw
   Marinated Italian Green
   Beans
   Macaroni "Lasagna"
   Skillet
   Lemon Fruit Tarts

4. Sweet Pickle Coleslaw
   Old-Time Green Bean
   Salad
   El Grande Potato Bake
   Banana Isle Pudding
   Desserts

5. Southern Belle Slaw
   Jiffy Tomato Soup
   Frankfurter Green Bean
   Bake
   Cherry-Chocolate
   Pudding Treats

6. Mediterranean Vegetable
   Salad
   Roman Holiday Tomato
   Rice Soup
   Zucchini-Pastrami Pasta
   Toss
   Lemon Cloud Fruit
   Dessert

7. Italian Radish and Pea
   Salad
   Neapolitan Corn
   Chowder
   Barbeque Tuna and
   Noodles
   Chocolate Strawberry
   Mud Pie

8. Garden Patch Salad
   Green Beans and
   Mushrooms
   Tuna Potato Bake
   Raspberry Chocolate
   Parfait

9. Provence Cucumber Salad
   Continental Green Beans
   Easy Fish Creole
   Graham Cracker
      Caribbean Dessert

10. Italian Tomato Mozzarella
       Salad
    Rice and Peas Side Dish
    Baked Fish Italian
    Fruit Cocktail Parfait

11. Mexican Bean Salad
    Adobe Vegetable Skillet
    Fiesta Burgers
    Hawaiian Banana Raisin
       Pie

12. Calico Cucumber Salad
    "Real Man" Gazpacho
    Tex-Mex Skillet Hash
    Yogurt Fruit Tarts

13. Italian Green Bean Salad
    Pineapple and Orange
       Cottage Salad
    Crunchy Loose Meat
       Sandwiches
    Caribbean Coconut
       Cheesecake

14. Broccoli Fruit Slaw
    Farmhouse Macaroni
       Bake
    Saucy "Faux" Steaks
    Chocolate Banana Sunset
       Pie

15. Cauliflower Pea Salad
    Easy Potato Salad
    Dill Cheeseburger Meat
       Loaf
    Summer Breeze Rice
       Pudding

16. Honey Dijon Cukes
    Salsa Pasta Salad
    Onion Meat Loaf
    Banana Boat Parfait

17. Layered Honey Dijon
       Tomato Salad
    Garden Patch Pea Salad
    Quick Turkey-'n'-Biscuits
    Butter Pecan Layered Pie

18. Sensational Pineapple
       Slaw
    Creamy Green Beans and
       Onions
    Veggie Turkey and
       Stuffing Skillet
    Pumpkin Pudding Parfait

19. Viva la Carrot Salad
    Thai Vegetable Pasta
       Salad
    Easy Glazed Chicken
    Layered Chocolate
       Raspberry Pie

20. Golden Broccoli Salad
    French Quarter Carrots
    Mex-Italian Chicken
       Skillet
    Grape Cream Pie

21. Dilly Veggie Salad
    Blushing Cauliflower
    Quickie Chicken Rice
        Skillet
    Warm Apple Banana Ice
        Cream Treats

22. Riviera Salad
    Tomato Patch Chicken
        Rice Soup
    Grilled Cheese and Ham
        Sandwich
    Tropical Pleasure Pie

23. Easy Coleslaw
    Green Beans and
        Pimiento Salad
    Creamy Chicken and
        Vegetable Skillet
    Hawaiian Pudding
        Dessert

24. Cabbage Angel Salad
    Grandma's "Baked" Beans
    BBQ Ham-Macaroni Salad
    Apricot-Pecan Tarts

25. Tropical Waldorf Salad
    Schnitzel Carrots
    Macaroni-Ham Skillet
    Cherry Cola Cheesecake

26. Chunky Carrot Salad
    Deli-Style Ham and
        Veggie Pizza
    Turtle Pie
    Lemon Orange Ade

27. California Ranch Corn
        Salad
    Sour Cream Cabbage
    Busy Day Pork Casserole
    Heavenly Orange Fluff

28. Carrot-Pea Salad
    Old-Fashioned Apple
        Salad
    Tomato Pork Stroganoff
    Apple-Cranberry Cider

29. Veggie Coleslaw
    Festive Pea Salad
    Hot Roast Beef
        Sandwiches
    Queen Anne's Cheesecake

30. Old-Time Spinach Salad
    Tomato and Cucumber
        Macaroni Salad
    Quick BBQ Beef
        Sandwiches
    Strawberry Lover's
        Pudding Treats

Menu 1

Mandarin Orange Spinach Salad
Calico Bean Salad
Cheesy Rice-Corn Skillet
Banana Lemon Cream Pie

*Here's a cheerful, colorful, and very satisfying meal that offers
lots of flavor for very little time in the kitchen! The spinach salad
dressing is citrusy and light, which is a nice balance alongside
the flavorful and filling bean dish. You can easily whip up the
side dishes and dessert while your skillet entree is simmering, so
dinner is ready in a snap of your fingers. Just think of all you'll
be able to do with the extra time!*

Mandarin Orange Spinach Salad

○ Serves 6 (1⅓ cups)

> 1 cup (one 11-ounce can) mandarin oranges, rinsed and drained
> 2 cups chopped fresh cauliflower
> ¼ cup chopped green bell pepper
> 2¾ cups fresh torn spinach leaves, stems discarded
> ¼ cup Kraft Fat Free Ranch Dressing
> ½ cup unsweetened orange juice
> 2 tablespoons Kraft fat-free mayonnaise

In a large bowl, combine mandarin oranges, cauliflower, green
pepper, and spinach leaves. In a small bowl, combine Ranch dressing, orange juice, and mayonnaise. Add dressing mixture to spinach
mixture. Toss gently to combine. Serve at once.

Each serving equals:

HE: 1⅔ Vegetable • ½ Fruit • ¼ Slider

60 Calories • 0 gm Fat • 2 gm Protein •
13 gm Carbohydrate • 171 mg Sodium • 2 gm Fiber

DIABETIC: 1 Vegetable • ½ Fruit

Calico Bean Salad

◑ Serves 6 (full ¾ cup)

10 ounces (one 16-ounce can) red kidney beans, rinsed and drained
1 cup frozen whole kernel corn, thawed
2 cups (one 16-ounce can) cut green beans, rinsed and drained
1 cup finely chopped celery
¼ cup Kraft Fat Free Italian Dressing
2 tablespoons Kraft fat-free mayonnaise
¼ cup (¾ ounce) grated Kraft fat-free Parmesan cheese
1 teaspoon dried parsley flakes
¼ teaspoon black pepper

In a large bowl, combine kidney beans, corn, green beans, and celery. In a small bowl, combine Italian dressing, mayonnaise, Parmesan cheese, parsley flakes, and black pepper. Add dressing mixture to vegetable mixture. Mix gently to combine. Cover and refrigerate for at least 15 minutes. Gently stir again just before serving.

HINT: Thaw corn by placing in a colander and rinsing under hot water for one minute.

Each serving equals:

HE: 1 Protein • 1 Vegetable • ⅓ Bread •
6 Optional Calories

92 Calories • 0 gm Fat • 5 gm Protein •
18 gm Carbohydrate • 103 mg Sodium • 6 gm Fiber

DIABETIC: 1 Vegetable • ½ Meat • ½ Starch

Cheesy Rice-Corn Skillet

● Serves 6 (1 cup)

1½ cups finely chopped celery
½ cup chopped onion
2 cups cold cooked rice
2 cups frozen whole kernel corn
⅔ cup Carnation Nonfat Dry Milk Powder
1 cup water
1½ cups (6 ounces) shredded Kraft reduced-fat Cheddar cheese
¼ cup (¾ ounce) grated Kraft fat-free Parmesan cheese
2 teaspoons dried parsley flakes
¼ teaspoon lemon pepper

In a large skillet sprayed with butter-flavored cooking spray, sauté celery and onion for 6 to 8 minutes or until just tender. Stir in rice and corn. In a small bowl, combine dry milk powder and water. Add milk mixture to the celery mixture. Mix well to combine. Stir Cheddar cheese, Parmesan cheese, parsley flakes, and lemon pepper into celery mixture. Lower heat and simmer for 10 minutes, stirring occasionally.

HINT: 1⅓ cups dry rice usually cooks to about 2 cups.

Each serving equals:

HE: 1½ Protein • 1⅓ Bread • ⅔ Vegetable •
⅓ Skim Milk

220 Calories • 4 gm Fat • 15 gm Protein •
31 gm Carbohydrate • 338 mg Sodium • 3 gm Fiber

DIABETIC: 1½ Meat • 1½ Starch • ½ Vegetable

Banana Lemon Cream Pie

○ Serves 8

3 cups (3 medium) finely diced bananas
1 (6-ounce) Keebler shortbread piecrust
1 (4-serving) package JELL-O sugar-free instant vanilla pudding
    mix
1 (4-serving) package JELL-O sugar-free lemon gelatin
⅔ cup Carnation Nonfat Dry Milk Powder
1⅓ cups Diet Mountain Dew
1 cup Cool Whip Lite☆
2 tablespoons (½ ounce) chopped pecans

Layer bananas in bottom of piecrust. In a large bowl, combine dry pudding mix, dry gelatin, dry milk powder, and Diet Mountain Dew. Mix well using a wire whisk. Blend in ¼ cup Cool Whip Lite. Spread pudding mixture evenly over bananas. Refrigerate 5 minutes. Evenly spread remaining ¾ cup Cool Whip Lite over set filling. Sprinkle pecans evenly over top. Refrigerate for at least 15 minutes. Cut into 8 servings.

HINT: To prevent bananas from turning brown, mix with 1 teaspoon lemon juice or sprinkle with Fruit Fresh.

Each serving equals:

HE: ¾ Fruit • ½ Bread • ¼ Skim Milk • ¼ Fat •
1 Slider • 7 Optional Calories

227 Calories • 7 gm Fat • 4 gm Protein •
37 gm Carbohydrate • 324 mg Sodium • 2 gm Fiber

DIABETIC: 1½ Starch • 1 Fruit • 1 Fat

Menu 2

Royal Carrot and Celery Salad
Home-Style Green Beans
Mexican Onion and Spaghetti Skillet
Chocolate Peppermint Pie

If you're tired of celery and carrot sticks, here's a delicious variation that delivers lots of vitamins in a crunchy mélange your whole family will love. For a chilly fall evening or any time you want to feel warm and cozy, this meal-in-a-skillet complements the creamy, cheesy green beans. Top off your meal with a fast and yummy pie that's both refreshing and fun, and you'll surely hear cheers all night long!

Royal Carrot and Celery Salad

- Serves 4 (¾ cup)

1½ cups shredded carrots
1 cup finely chopped celery
2 tablespoons (½ ounce) chopped walnuts
⅓ cup Kraft fat-free mayonnaise
1 teaspoon lemon juice
Sugar substitute to equal 2 teaspoons sugar
Lettuce leaves

In a medium bowl, combine carrots, celery, and walnuts. In a small bowl, combine mayonnaise, lemon juice, and sugar substitute. Add mayonnaise mixture to carrot mixture. Mix well to combine.

Cover and refrigerate for at least 20 minutes. Gently stir again just before serving. Serve on lettuce leaves.

Each serving equals:

HE: 1¼ Vegetable • ¼ Fat • ¼ Slider

58 Calories • 2 gm Fat • 1 gm Protein •
9 gm Carbohydrate • 182 mg Sodium • 2 gm Fiber

DIABETIC: 2 Vegetable

Home-Style Green Beans ❄

○ Serves 4 (1 cup)

4 cups (two 16-ounce cans) cut green beans, rinsed and drained
1 tablespoon dried onion flakes
2 tablespoons Hormel Bacon Bits
1 (10¾-ounce) can Healthy Request Cream of Mushroom Soup
¼ teaspoon black pepper
⅓ cup (1½ ounces) shredded Kraft reduced-fat Cheddar cheese

In a large skillet, combine green beans, onion flakes, and bacon bits. Cook over medium heat, stirring occasionally, for 5 minutes or until mixture is warmed through. Add mushroom soup, black pepper, and Cheddar cheese. Mix well to combine. Lower heat and simmer for 5 minutes or until cheese melts, stirring occasionally.

Each serving equals:

HE: 2 Vegetable • ½ Protein • ½ Slider •
14 Optional Calories

124 Calories • 4 gm Fat • 7 gm Protein •
15 gm Carbohydrate • 469 mg Sodium • 2 gm Fiber

DIABETIC: 2 Vegetable • ½ Meat • ½ Fat

Mexican Onion and Spaghetti Skillet

◐ Serves 4 (1 cup)

> 3 cups sliced onion
>
> 1½ cups (one 12-fluid-ounce can) Carnation Evaporated Skim
> Milk
>
> 3 tablespoons all-purpose flour
>
> ¼ teaspoon lemon pepper
>
> 1 teaspoon dried parsley flakes
>
> ¾ cup (3 ounces) shredded Kraft reduced-fat Cheddar cheese
>
> ½ cup chunky salsa (mild, medium, or hot)
>
> 1½ cups hot cooked spaghetti, rinsed and drained

In a large skillet sprayed with butter-flavored cooking spray, sauté onion for 10 minutes or until tender. In a covered jar, combine evaporated skim milk, flour, lemon pepper, and parsley flakes. Shake well to blend. Pour milk mixture into skillet with onion. Add Cheddar cheese, salsa, and spaghetti. Mix well to combine. Lower heat and simmer for 10 minutes, stirring often.

Each serving equals:

HE: 1¾ Vegetable • 1 Protein • 1 Bread • ¾ Skim Milk

264 Calories • 4 gm Fat • 18 gm Protein •
39 gm Carbohydrate • 389 mg Sodium • 3 gm Fiber

DIABETIC: 1½ Vegetable • 1 Meat • 1 Starch •
1 Skim Milk

Chocolate Peppermint Pie

○ Serves 8

1 (4-serving) package JELL-O sugar-free instant chocolate
    pudding mix
⅔ cup Carnation Nonfat Dry Milk Powder
1¼ cups water
1 cup Cool Whip Lite☆
1 (6 ounce) Keebler chocolate piecrust
¾ teaspoon mint extract
3 to 4 drops green food coloring
1 tablespoon (¼ ounce) mini chocolate chips

In a medium bowl, combine dry pudding mix, dry milk powder, and water. Mix well using a wire whisk. Blend in ¼ cup Cool
Whip Lite. Spread mixture evenly into piecrust. Refrigerate while
preparing topping. In a small bowl, combine remaining ¾ cup Cool
Whip Lite, mint extract, and green food coloring. Spread topping
mixture evenly over pudding mixture. Sprinkle chocolate chips
evenly over top. Refrigerate for at least 20 minutes. Cut into 8 servings.

Each serving equals:

HE: ½ Bread • ¼ Skim Milk • 1 Slider •

10 Optional Calories

_____

166 Calories • 6 gm Fat • 4 gm Protein •

24 gm Carbohydrate • 296 mg Sodium • 1 gm Fiber

_____

DIABETIC: 1½ Starch *or* Carbohydrate • 1 Fat

Menu 3

Cabbage Patch Slaw
Marinated Italian Green Beans
Macaroni "Lasagna" Skillet
Lemon Fruit Tarts

What's the difference between a meal that's just "okay" and a feast that feeds the soul? Texture and flavor—like the fresh crunch of a traditional coleslaw, and the taste surprises in a simple skillet lasagna that's as scrumptious and saucy as it is healthy and quick to stir up! Individual lemon "cheesecakes" bring your meal to a supremely satisfying finale!

Cabbage Patch Slaw

○ Serves 4 (¾ cup)

3 cups shredded cabbage
¾ cup shredded carrots
½ cup finely diced celery
¼ cup finely diced onion
½ cup Kraft fat-free mayonnaise
¼ teaspoon lemon pepper
2 teaspoons prepared horseradish
Sugar substitute to equal 2 tablespoons sugar
1 tablespoon white vinegar
1 teaspoon celery seed

In a medium bowl, combine cabbage, carrots, celery, and onion. In a small bowl, combine mayonnaise, lemon pepper, horseradish, sugar substitute, vinegar, and celery seed. Add mayonnaise mixture to cabbage mixture. Mix well to combine. Cover and refrigerate for at least 20 minutes. Gently stir again just before serving.

HINT: 3¾ cups purchased coleslaw mix may be used in place of cabbage and carrots.

Each serving equals:

HE: 2¼ Vegetable • ¼ Slider • 4 Optional Calories

52 Calories • 0 gm Fat • 1 gm Protein •
12 gm Carbohydrate • 245 mg Sodium • 2 Fiber

DIABETIC: 2 Vegetable

Marinated Italian Green Beans

○ Serves 4 (½ cup)

2 cups (one 16-ounce can) Italian green beans, rinsed and
drained
½ cup finely chopped onion
¼ cup Kraft Fat Free Italian Dressing

In a medium bowl, combine green beans and onion. Add Italian dressing. Toss gently to combine. Cover and refrigerate for at least 20 minutes. Gently stir again just before serving.

Each serving equals:

HE: 1¼ Vegetable • 4 Optional Calories

32 Calories • 0 gm Fat • 1 gm Protein •
7 gm Carbohydrate • 144 mg Sodium • 2 gm Fiber

DIABETIC: 1 Vegetable

Macaroni "Lasagna" Skillet

○ Serves 4

> 1¾ cups (one 15-ounce can) Hunt's Chunky Tomato Sauce
> ¼ teaspoon dried minced garlic
> 1 teaspoon Italian seasoning
> 1 teaspoon dried parsley flakes
> ¼ teaspoon black pepper
> 1 cup fat-free cottage cheese
> 1½ cups (6 ounces) shredded Kraft reduced-fat mozzarella cheese☆
> ¼ cup (¾ ounce) grated Kraft fat-free Parmesan cheese
> 2 cups hot cooked macaroni, rinsed and drained

In a large skillet sprayed with olive oil–flavored cooking spray, combine tomato sauce, garlic, Italian seasoning, parsley flakes, and black pepper. Bring mixture to a boil. Add cottage cheese, 1 cup mozzarella cheese and Parmesan cheese. Mix well to combine. Continue cooking for 5 minutes or until the cheeses begin to melt, stirring often. Stir in macaroni. Evenly sprinkle remaining ½ cup mozzarella cheese over top. Lower heat, cover, and simmer for 5 minutes or until mozzarella cheese melts. Divide into 4 (1-cup) servings.

HINT: 1⅓ cups uncooked macaroni usually cooks to about 2 cups.

Each serving equals:

HE: 2¾ Protein • 1¾ Vegetable • 1 Bread

282 Calories • 6 gm Fat • 28 gm Protein •
29 gm Carbohydrate • 976 mg Sodium • 1 gm Fiber

DIABETIC: 3 Meat • 1½ Vegetable • 1½ Starch

Lemon Fruit Tarts

○ Serves 6

1 (8-ounce) package Philadelphia fat-free cream cheese
1 (4-serving) package JELL-O sugar-free lemon gelatin
½ cup Cool Whip Lite
1 (6-single serve) package Keebler graham cracker crusts
6 tablespoons spreadable fruit spread (any flavor)

In a medium bowl, stir cream cheese with a spoon until soft. Add dry gelatin and Cool Whip Lite. Continue stirring until well blended. Evenly spread cream cheese mixture into graham cracker crusts. Spread 1 tablespoon spreadable fruit over top of each. Refrigerate for at least 15 minutes.

HINT: Spreadable fruit spreads best at room temperature.

Each serving equals:

HE: 1 Fruit • ⅔ Protein • ½ Bread • ¾ Slider •
10 Optional Calories

194 Calories • 6 gm Fat • 7 gm Protein •
28 gm Carbohydrate • 408 mg Sodium • 0 gm Fiber

DIABETIC: 1 Fruit • 1 Fat • 1 Starch

Menu 4

Sweet Pickle Coleslaw
Old-Time Green Bean Salad
El Grande Potato Bake
Banana Isle Pudding Desserts

I took a picnic taste we all love—sweet pickle relish—and stirred it into a speedy coleslaw you won't save just for family outings anymore. Add a side salad that sparkles with bits of bacon, a main-dish Mexican casserole that'll fill up the hungriest tummy, and a sweet taste of paradise in a dessert dish for a meal that feels more like a party!

Sweet Pickle Coleslaw

● Serves 4 (⅔ cup)

2 tablespoons sweet pickle relish
½ teaspoon celery seed
⅓ cup Kraft fat-free mayonnaise
3 cups purchased coleslaw mix

In a medium bowl, combine sweet pickle relish, celery seed, and mayonnaise. Add coleslaw mix. Mix well to combine. Cover and refrigerate for at least 20 minutes. Gently stir again just before serving.

HINT: 2½ cups shredded cabbage and ½ cup shredded carrots may be used instead of purchased coleslaw mix.

Each serving equals:

HE: 1½ Vegetable • 14 Optional Calories

40 Calories • 0 gm Fat • 1 gm Protein •
9 gm Carbohydrate • 206 mg Sodium • 1 gm Fiber

DIABETIC: 1½ Vegetable

Old-Time Green Bean Salad

○ Serves 4 (¾ cup)

> 4 cups (two 16-ounce cans) cut green beans, rinsed and drained
> 1 hard-boiled egg, chopped
> 1 tablespoon Hormel Bacon Bits
> ¼ cup dill pickle relish
> 1 teaspoon dried parsley flakes
> 1 teaspoon prepared mustard
> ¼ teaspoon black pepper
> ¼ cup Kraft fat-free mayonnaise

In a medium bowl, combine green beans, egg, and bacon bits. In a small bowl, combine dill pickle relish, parsley flakes, mustard, black pepper, and mayonnaise. Add dressing mixture to green bean mixture. Mix gently to combine. Cover and refrigerate for at least 20 minutes. Gently stir again just before serving.

HINT: If you want the look and feel of eggs without the cholesterol, toss out the yolk and dice the whites.

Each serving equals:

HE: 2 Vegetable • ¼ Protein (limited) •
16 Optional Calories

90 Calories • 2 gm Fat • 4 gm Protein •
14 gm Carbohydrate • 285 mg Sodium • 3 gm Fiber

DIABETIC: 2 Vegetable • ½ Fat

El Grande Potato Bake ❄

○ Serves 4

   1⅔ cups water

   ¼ cup finely chopped onion

   1 cup (3 ounces) instant potato flakes

   ⅓ cup Carnation Nonfat Dry Milk Powder

   1 teaspoon taco seasoning mix

   10 ounces (one 16-ounce can) red kidney beans, rinsed and
      drained

   1¾ cups (one 14½-ounce can) stewed tomatoes, coarsely chopped
      and undrained

   ¾ cup (3 ounces) shredded Kraft reduced-fat Cheddar cheese

   1 teaspoon dried parsley flakes

Preheat oven to 350 degrees. Spray an 8-by-8-inch baking dish with olive oil–flavored cooking spray. In a medium saucepan, combine water and onion. Cook over medium heat until mixture starts to boil. Remove from heat. Stir in potato flakes, dry milk powder, and taco seasoning mix. Add kidney beans. Mix well to combine. Spread mixture evenly into prepared baking dish. Evenly spread undrained stewed tomatoes over potato mixture. Sprinkle Cheddar cheese and parsley flakes over top. Bake for 20 minutes. Place baking dish on a wire rack and let set for 5 minutes. Divide into 4 servings.

Each serving equals:

HE: 2¼ Protein • 1 Bread • 1 Vegetable • ¼ Skim Milk

211 Calories • 3 gm Fat • 14 gm Protein •
32 gm Carbohydrate • 493 mg Sodium • 7 mg Fiber

DIABETIC: 2 Starch • 1½ Meat • 1 Vegetable

Banana Isle Pudding Desserts

● Serves 4

1 (4-serving) package JELL-O sugar-free instant banana pudding
   mix

⅔ cup Carnation Nonfat Dry Milk Powder

1 cup water

1 cup (one 8-ounce can) crushed pineapple, packed in fruit juice,
   undrained

1 cup (1 medium) diced banana

½ cup Cool Whip Lite☆

½ teaspoon apple pie spice

In a large bowl, combine dry pudding mix, dry milk powder, and water. Mix well using a wire whisk. Stir in undrained pineapple and banana. Add ¼ cup Cool Whip Lite and apple pie spice. Mix well to combine. Spoon mixture into 4 dessert dishes. Refrigerate for at least 20 minutes. When serving, top each with 1 tablespoon Cool Whip Lite.

HINT: To prevent banana from turning brown, mix with 1 teaspoon lemon juice or sprinkle with Fruit Fresh.

Each serving equals:

HE: 1 Fruit • ½ Skim Milk • ½ Slider •
5 Optional Calories

157 Calories • 1 gm Fat • 5 gm Protein •
32 gm Carbohydrate • 403 mg Sodium • 1 gm Fiber

DIABETIC: 1 Fruit • ½ Starch • ½ Skim Milk

Menu 5

Southern Belle Slaw
Jiffy Tomato Soup
Frankfurter Green Bean Bake
Cherry-Chocolate Pudding Treats

Remember when your mom served you tomato soup and frankfurters, and you knew how much she loved you? Here's a menu that re-creates those cozy memories: the creamiest healthy tomato soup you may ever savor, a tangy "franks and beans" dish that's all grown-up, a sweet slaw that nearly explodes with crunchy flavor, and a chocolatey dessert that tastes like a reward for being really good. Enjoy!

Southern Belle Slaw

○ Serves 4 (full ½ cup)

> 2 cups purchased coleslaw mix
> 1 cup (one 11-ounce can) mandarin oranges, rinsed and drained
> 2 tablespoons (½ ounce) chopped pecans
> ½ cup Kraft fat-free mayonnaise
> 2 tablespoons Cary's Sugar Free Maple Syrup

In a large bowl, combine coleslaw mix, mandarin oranges, and pecans. In a small bowl, combine mayonnaise and maple syrup. Add mayonnaise mixture to coleslaw mixture. Toss gently to combine. Cover and refrigerate for at least 20 minutes. Gently stir again just before serving.

HINT: 1½ cups shredded cabbage and ½ cup shredded carrots may be used in place of purchased coleslaw mix.

Each serving equals:

HE: 1 Vegetable • ½ Fat • ½ Fruit • ¼ Slider •
5 Optional Calories

78 Calories • 2 gm Fat • 1 gm Protein •
14 gm Carbohydrate • 233 mg Sodium • 1 gm Fiber

DIABETIC: 1 Vegetable • ½ Fat • ½ Fruit

Jiffy Tomato Soup

◉ Serves 4 (1 cup)

1¾ cups (one 15-ounce can) Hunt's Chunky Tomato Sauce
1 (10¾-ounce) can Healthy Request Tomato Soup
½ teaspoon baking soda
2 teaspoons Sugar Twin or Sprinkle Sweet
1½ cups (one 12-fluid-ounce can) Carnation Evaporated Skim
   Milk
½ teaspoon black pepper
1 teaspoon chili seasoning mix

In a medium saucepan, combine tomato sauce and tomato soup. Cook over medium heat until mixture starts to boil, stirring often. Stir in baking soda, Sugar Twin, evaporated skim milk, black pepper, and chili seasoning mix. Lower heat and simmer for 5 minutes or until mixture is heated through, stirring constantly.

Each serving equals:

HE: 1¾ Vegetable • ¾ Skim Milk • ½ Slider •
6 Optional Calories

157 Calories • 1 gm Fat • 9 gm Protein •
28 gm Carbohydrate • 957 mg Sodium • 3 gm Fiber

DIABETIC: 2 Vegetable • 1 Skim Milk

Frankfurter Green Bean Bake ❄

○ Serves 4

½ cup chopped onion

8 ounces Healthy Choice 97% fat-free frankfurters, diced

4 cups (two 16-ounce cans) cut green beans, rinsed and drained

1¾ cups (one 15-ounce can) Hunt's Chunky Tomato Sauce

1 teaspoon prepared mustard

2 tablespoons Brown Sugar Twin

¼ teaspoon black pepper

Preheat oven to 350 degrees. Spray an 8-by-8-inch baking dish with butter-flavored cooking spray. In a large skillet sprayed with butter-flavored cooking spray, sauté onion and frankfurters for 5 minutes or until onion is tender. Stir in green beans and tomato sauce. Add mustard, Brown Sugar Twin, and black pepper. Mix well to combine. Pour mixture into prepared baking dish. Bake for 20 to 25 minutes. Place baking dish on a wire rack and let set for 5 minutes. Divide into 4 servings.

HINT: 1½ cups (8 ounces) diced Dubuque 97% fat-free ham or any extra-lean ham may be used in place of frankfurters.

Each serving equals:

HE: 4 Vegetable • 1⅓ Protein • 2 Optional Calories

129 Calories • 1 gm Fat • 11 gm Protein •
19 gm Carbohydrate • 995 mg Sodium • 2 gm Fiber

DIABETIC: 4 Vegetable • 1 Meat *or*
1 Starch • 1 Vegetable • 1 Meat

Cherry-Chocolate
Pudding Treats

● Serves 4

1 (4-serving) package JELL-O sugar-free instant chocolate
   pudding mix
⅔ cup Carnation Nonfat Dry Milk Powder
1½ cups water
¼ cup black cherry spreadable fruit spread
¼ cup Cool Whip Lite
4 teaspoons (⅓ ounce) chopped walnuts

In a medium bowl, combine dry pudding mix, dry milk powder, and water. Mix well using a wire whisk. Evenly spoon mixture into four dessert dishes. Refrigerate while preparing topping. In a small bowl, combine spreadable fruit and Cool Whip Lite. Mix gently to combine. Spoon mixture evenly over top of pudding. Sprinkle 1 teaspoon walnuts evenly over top of each. Refrigerate for at least 15 minutes.

Each serving equals:

HE: 1 Fruit • ½ Skim Milk • ½ Slider •
12 Optional Calories

146 Calories • 2 gm Fat • 5 gm Protein •
27 gm Carbohydrate • 408 mg Sodium • 0 gm Fiber

DIABETIC: 1 Fruit • ½ Skim Milk • ½ Starch

Mediterranean Vegetable Salad

◐ Serves 4 (full ¾ cup)

> 2 cups chopped fresh tomatoes
> 1 cup unpeeled chopped cucumbers
> ⅓ cup (1½ ounces) shredded Kraft reduced-fat mozzarella cheese
> 1 tablespoon chopped fresh parsley or 1 teaspoon dried parsley
>   flakes
> ¼ cup Kraft Fat Free Italian Dressing

In a large bowl, combine tomatoes, cucumbers, mozzarella
cheese, and parsley. Add Italian dressing. Mix gently to combine.
Cover and refrigerate for at least 20 minutes. Gently stir again just
before serving.

Each serving equals:

HE: 1½ Vegetable • ½ Protein • 4 Optional Calories

58 Calories • 2 gm Fat • 4 gm Protein •
6 gm Carbohydrate • 259 mg Sodium • 1 gm Fiber

DIABETIC: 1 Vegetable • ½ Fat

Roman Holiday Tomato Rice Soup

○ Serves 4 (1½ cups)

½ cup finely chopped onion
½ cup finely chopped green bell pepper
4 cups (two 16-ounce cans) tomatoes, coarsely chopped and
    undrained
1 cup water
2 teaspoons Italian seasoning
⅛ teaspoon black pepper
¼ cup (1 ounce) sliced ripe olives
⅓ cup (2 ounces) chopped Canadian bacon or any extra-lean
    ham
⅔ cup (2 ounces) uncooked instant rice

In a large saucepan sprayed with olive oil–flavored cooking spray, sauté onion and green pepper for 5 minutes or until tender. Meanwhile, place undrained tomatoes in a blender container. Cover and process on BLEND for 30 seconds. Add pureed tomatoes and water into saucepan with onion and green pepper. Mix well to combine. Stir in Italian seasoning, black pepper, olives, and Canadian bacon. Bring mixture to a boil. Stir in rice. Remove from heat, cover, and let set for 5 minutes. Stir again just before serving.

Each serving equals:

HE: 2½ Vegetable • ½ Protein • ½ Bread • ¼ Fat

110 Calories • 2 gm Fat • 5 gm Protein •
18 gm Carbohydrate • 291 mg Sodium • 3 gm Fiber

DIABETIC: 2 Vegetable • ½ Meat • ½ Starch

Zucchini-Pastrami Pasta Toss ❄

● Serves 4 (full 1 cup)

> 2 cups unpeeled sliced zucchini
> 2 (2.5-ounce) packages Carl Buddig lean pastrami
> 1¾ cups (one 15-ounce can) Hunt's Chunky Tomato Sauce
> 1½ teaspoons Italian seasoning
> ¼ cup (¾ ounce) grated Kraft fat-free Parmesan cheese
> 2 cups hot cooked rotini pasta, rinsed and drained

In a large skillet sprayed with olive oil–flavored cooking spray, sauté zucchini and pastrami for 5 minutes or until lightly browned. Add tomato sauce and Italian seasoning. Mix well to combine. Stir in Parmesan cheese and rotini pasta. Lower heat and simmer for 10 minutes or until mixture is heated through, stirring occasionally.

HINTS: 1. 1½ cups uncooked rotini pasta usually cooks to about 2 cups.

2. Garden Variety Rotini pasta works great.

Each serving equals:

HE: 2¾ Vegetable • 1½ Protein • 1 Bread

203 Calories • 3 gm Fat • 14 gm Protein •
30 gm Carbohydrate • 1060 mg Sodium • 2 gm Fiber

DIABETIC: 3 Vegetable • 1½ Meat • 1 Starch

Lemon Cloud Fruit Dessert

○ Serves 4

> 1 (4-serving) package JELL-O sugar-free instant vanilla pudding mix
> 1 (4-serving) package JELL-O sugar-free lemon gelatin
> ⅔ cup Carnation Nonfat Dry Milk Powder
> 2 cups (one 16-ounce can) fruit cocktail, packed in fruit juice, drained, and ½ cup liquid reserved
> 1 cup water
> ½ cup Cool Whip Lite
> ½ cup (1 ounce) miniature marshmallows

In a medium bowl, combine dry pudding mix, dry gelatin, and dry milk powder. Add reserved fruit cocktail liquid and water. Mix well using a wire whisk. Blend in Cool Whip Lite, drained fruit cocktail, and marshmallows. Evenly spoon mixture into 4 dessert dishes. Refrigerate for at least 15 minutes.

Each serving equals:

HE: 1 Fruit • ½ Skim Milk • ½ Slider • 15 Optional Calories

169 Calories • 1 gm Fat • 6 gm Protein • 34 gm Carbohydrate • 453 mg Sodium • 1 gm Fiber

DIABETIC: 1 Starch *or* Carbohydrate • 1 Fruit

Menu 7

Italian Radish and Pea Salad
Neapolitan Corn Chowder
Barbeque Tuna and Noodles
Chocolate Strawberry Mud Pie

Well-spiced food that's full of flavor makes dining low-fat a symphony of satisfaction in these nontraditional "traditional" combinations! The colors are as bright as a picture postcard, from the salad's red, white, and green (Italy's flag colors) to the golden yellow of a hearty corn chowder. Follow that with a speedy tuna skillet and a mud pie both berry sweet and chocolate fudgy, and you've got a recipe for pleasure that ought to win a medal!

Italian Radish and Pea Salad

◑ Serves 4 (²/₃ cup)

> 2 cups frozen peas, thawed
> ½ cup finely chopped radishes
> ½ cup Kraft Fat Free Italian Dressing

In a medium bowl, combine peas and radishes. Add Italian dressing. Mix gently to combine. Cover and refrigerate for at least 20 minutes. Gently stir again just before serving.

HINT: Thaw peas by placing in a colander and rinsing under hot water for one minute.

Each serving equals:

HE: 1 Bread • ¼ Vegetable • 8 Optional Calories

68 Calories • 0 gm Fat • 4 gm Protein •
13 gm Carbohydrate • 287 mg Sodium • 4 gm Fiber

DIABETIC: 1 Starch

Neapolitan Corn Chowder

☉ Serves 4 (1½ cups)

2 cups (10 ounces) diced raw potatoes
2 cups (one 16-ounce can) Healthy Request Chicken Broth
1 cup frozen whole kernel corn
1¾ cups (one 15-ounce can) Hunt's Chunky Tomato Sauce
½ cup (one 2.5-ounce jar) sliced mushrooms, drained
1 teaspoon Italian seasoning
2 teaspoons Sugar Twin or Sprinkle Sweet
½ teaspoon dried minced garlic
2 teaspoons dried parsley flakes

In a medium saucepan, combine potatoes and chicken broth.
Cook over medium heat for 10 minutes or until potatoes are tender.
Add corn, tomato sauce, mushrooms, Italian seasoning, Sugar Twin,
garlic, and parsley flakes. Bring mixture to a boil. Lower heat and
simmer for about 10 minutes, stirring occasionally.

Each serving equals:

HE: 2 Vegetable • 1 Bread • 9 Optional Calories

132 Calories • 0 gm Fat • 6 gm Protein •
27 gm Carbohydrate • 832 mg Sodium • 1 gm Fiber

DIABETIC: 2 Vegetable • 1 Starch

Barbeque Tuna and Noodles ❄

● Serves 4 (1 cup)

½ cup chopped green bell pepper

½ cup chopped onion

1 teaspoon Worcestershire sauce

1¾ cups (one 15-ounce can) Hunt's Chunky Tomato Sauce

1 tablespoon Brown Sugar Twin

1 teaspoon chili seasoning mix

1 tablespoon white vinegar

1 (6-ounce) can white tuna, packed in water, drained and flaked

2 cups hot cooked noodles, rinsed and drained

In a large skillet sprayed with butter-flavored cooking spray, sauté green pepper and onion for 6 to 8 minutes or until tender. Stir in Worcestershire sauce, tomato sauce, Brown Sugar Twin, chili seasoning mix, and vinegar. Add tuna and noodles. Mix well to combine. Lower heat and simmer for 10 minutes or until mixture is heated through, stirring occasionally.

HINT: 1¾ cups uncooked noodles usually cooks to about 2 cups.

Each serving equals:

HE: 2¼ Vegetable • ¾ Protein • 1 Bread •
1 Optional Calorie

194 Calories • 2 gm Fat • 16 gm Protein •
28 gm Carbohydrate • 864 mg Sodium • 2 gm Fiber

DIABETIC: 1½ Vegetable • 1½ Meat • 1 Starch

Chocolate Strawberry Mud Pie

● Serves 8

> 2 cups sliced fresh strawberries
> 1 (6-ounce) Keebler chocolate piecrust
> 1 (4-serving) package JELL-O sugar-free instant chocolate
>   pudding mix
> ⅔ cup Carnation Nonfat Dry Milk Powder
> 1¼ cups water
> ¾ cup Cool Whip Lite☆
> 1 teaspoon almond extract☆
> 2 tablespoons (½ ounce) finely chopped slivered almonds
> 2 teaspoons chocolate syrup

Layer strawberries in bottom of piecrust. In a large bowl, combine dry pudding mix, dry milk powder and water. Mix well using a wire whisk. Blend in ¼ cup Cool Whip Lite and ½ teaspoon almond extract. Spread pudding mixture evenly over strawberries. Refrigerate while preparing topping. In a small bowl, gently combine remaining ½ cup Cool Whip Lite, remaining ½ teaspoon almond extract and almonds. Spread topping mixture evenly over set filling. Drizzle chocolate syrup evenly over the top. Refrigerate for at least 15 minutes. Cut into 8 servings.

Each serving equals:

HE: ½ Bread • ¼ Fruit • ¼ Skim Milk • ¼ Fat •
1 Slider • 6 Optional Calories

183 Calories • 7 gm Fat • 4 gm Protein •
26 gm Carbohydrate • 298 mg Sodium • 1 gm Fiber

DIABETIC: 2 Starch or Carbohydrate • 1 Fat

Menu 8

Garden Patch Salad
Green Beans and Mushrooms
Tuna Potato Bake
Raspberry Chocolate Parfait

When the harvest is at its ripest, here's a menu to celebrate a couple of farmers' market specials: a colorful salad that shares all the joys of the garden and a dessert that promises perfection as only the taste of a ripe raspberry can! Add these seasonal treats to a quick-and-easy tuna bake that sizzles with pizazz and a cozy, creamy green bean dish, and you'll be ready to dance the night away under a shimmering harvest moon. Shine on!

Garden Patch Salad

○ Serves 4 (1 cup)

> ½ cup unpeeled diced zucchini
> 1 cup diced fresh tomatoes
> ½ cup diced green bell pepper
> ½ cup diced onion
> ½ cup chopped radishes
> ½ cup thinly sliced carrots
> ½ cup thinly sliced celery
> ¼ cup Kraft Fat Free French Dressing
> 2 tablespoons Kraft Fat Free Italian Dressing
> 1 tablespoon fresh parsley or 1 teaspoon dried parsley flakes

In a large bowl, combine zucchini, tomatoes, green pepper, onion, radishes, carrots, and celery. In a small bowl, combine

French dressing, Italian dressing, and parsley. Pour dressing mixture over vegetables. Mix gently to combine. Cover and refrigerate for at least 20 minutes. Gently stir again just before serving.

Each serving equals:

HE: 2 Vegetable • ¼ Slider • 7 Optional Calories

52 Calories • 0 gm Fat • 1 gm Protein •
12 gm Carbohydrate • 217 mg Sodium • 2 gm Fiber

DIABETIC: 2 Vegetable

Green Beans and Mushrooms

○ Serves 4 (¾ cup)

½ cup chopped onion
1½ cups sliced fresh mushrooms
¼ cup (1 ounce) slivered almonds
1 (10¾-ounce) can Healthy Request Cream of Mushroom Soup
4 cups (two 16-ounce cans) cut green beans, rinsed and drained
¼ teaspoon black pepper

In a large skillet sprayed with butter-flavored cooking spray, sauté onion for 5 minutes or until tender. Add mushrooms and almonds. Mix well to combine. Continue cooking, stirring often, for 2 to 3 minutes. Stir in mushroom soup, green beans, and black pepper. Lower heat and simmer for 5 minutes or until mixture is heated through, stirring occasionally.

Each serving equals:

HE: 3 Vegetable • ½ Fat • ¼ Protein • ½ Slider •
1 Optional Calorie

125 Calories • 5 gm Fat • 4 gm Protein •
16 gm Carbohydrate • 323 mg Sodium • 4 gm Fiber

DIABETIC: 2 Vegetable • 1 Fat • ½ Starch

Tuna Potato Bake

● Serves 4

1⅔ cups water

1⅓ cups (3 ounces) instant potato flakes

⅓ cup Carnation Nonfat Dry Milk Powder

¾ cup Yoplait plain fat-free yogurt

2 tablespoons Kraft fat-free mayonnaise

¼ teaspoon black pepper

1 teaspoon dried parsley flakes

1 teaspoon chili seasoning mix

1 (9½-ounce) can white tuna, packed in water, drained and
    flaked

¾ cup (3 ounces) shredded Kraft reduced-fat Cheddar cheese

½ cup chopped green bell pepper

Spray an 8-by-8-inch glass baking dish with butter-flavored cooking spray. In an 8-cup glass measuring bowl, microwave water on HIGH (100% power) until water starts to boil, about 2 minutes. Add potato flakes and dry milk powder. Mix well to combine. Let cool for 2 to 3 minutes. Stir in yogurt, mayonnaise, black pepper, parsley flakes, and chili seasoning mix. Add tuna, Cheddar cheese, and green pepper. Mix well to combine. Spread mixture into prepared baking dish. Cover with waxed paper. Microwave on HIGH for 6 minutes, turning after 3 minutes. Place baking dish on a wire rack and let set for 3 to 5 minutes. Divide into 4 servings.

Each serving equals:

HE: 2 Protein • 1 Bread • ½ Skim Milk • ¼ Vegetable •
5 Optional Calories

236 Calories • 4 gm Fat • 29 gm Protein •
21 gm Carbohydrate • 525 mg Sodium • 1 gm Fiber

DIABETIC: 3 Meat • 1 Starch • ½ Skim Milk

Raspberry Chocolate Parfait

● Serves 4

> 1 (4-serving) package JELL-O sugar-free instant chocolate
>   pudding mix
> ⅓ cup Carnation Nonfat Dry Milk Powder
> 1½ cups Yoplait plain fat-free yogurt
> ½ cup water
> ½ teaspoon almond extract
> 6 tablespoons purchased graham cracker crumbs or six
>   (2½-inch) squares made into crumbs☆
> ¾ cup fresh red raspberries
> ¼ cup Cool Whip Lite

In a medium bowl, combine dry pudding mix and dry milk powder. Add yogurt and water. Mix well using a wire whisk. Blend in almond extract. Spoon about ¼ cup pudding mixture into 4 parfait or dessert dishes. Sprinkle about 1 tablespoon graham cracker crumbs over top of each. Reserve 4 raspberries. Evenly divide remaining raspberries among the four dishes. Evenly spoon remaining chocolate pudding (about ¼ cup each) over raspberries. Top each with 1 tablespoon Cool Whip Lite. Sprinkle about 1½ teaspoons crumbs over top of each and garnish with 1 reserved raspberry. Refrigerate for at least 15 minutes.

HINT: Frozen unsweetened raspberries, thawed and drained, may
    be substituted for fresh.

Each serving equals:

HE: ¾ Skim Milk • ½ Bread • ¼ Fruit • ½ Slider

174 Calories • 2 gm Fat • 9 gm Protein •
30 gm Carbohydrate • 493 mg Sodium • 1 gm Fiber

DIABETIC: 1 Skim Milk • 1 Carbohydrate • ½ Fat

Menu 9

Provence Cucumber Salad
Continental Green Beans
Easy Fish Creole
Graham Cracker Caribbean Dessert

Even if you "eat to live" instead of "live to eat," good-tasting healthy recipes are an important part of what makes life worth living! How about a luscious fish dish that smells so good your family will keep peeking into the kitchen to ask when dinner will be ready. Couple it with a creamy cuke salad, a delectable blend of green beans and Ranch dressing served tangy-hot, and a sweet taste of the tropics for dessert. Then stand back and enjoy the applause—you deserve it!

Provence Cucumber Salad

● Serves 4 (½ cup)

¼ cup Kraft Fat Free French Dressing
1 tablespoon Kraft fat-free mayonnaise
1 tablespoon Dijon mustard
2 tablespoons chopped fresh parsley or 1 teaspoon dried parsley
    flakes
2¼ cups unpeeled thinly sliced cucumbers
¼ cup finely chopped onion

In a medium bowl, combine French dressing, mayonnaise, mustard, and parsley. Add cucumbers and onion. Mix gently to combine. Cover and refrigerate for at least 20 minutes. Gently stir again just before serving.

Each serving equals:

HE: 1¼ Vegetable • ¼ Slider • 13 Optional Calories

28 Calories • 0 gm Fat • 0 gm Protein •
7 gm Carbohydrate • 149 mg Sodium • 1 gm Fiber

DIABETIC: 1 Vegetable

Continental Green Beans

• Serves 4 (full ¾ cup)

⅓ cup Kraft Fat Free Ranch Dressing
1 tablespoon dried minced onion
¼ teaspoon dried minced garlic
1 teaspoon Italian seasoning
4 cups (two 16-ounce cans) cut green beans, rinsed and drained

In a large saucepan, combine Ranch dressing, onion, garlic, and Italian seasoning. Mix well to combine. Stir in green beans. Cook over medium heat for 10 minutes or until mixture is heated through, stirring often.

Each serving equals:

HE: 2 Vegetable • ¼ Slider • 13 Optional Calories

64 Calories • 0 gm Fat • 2 gm Protein •
14 gm Carbohydrate • 165 mg Sodium • 4 gm Fiber

DIABETIC: 2 Vegetable

Easy Fish Creole

● Serves 4

½ cup chopped onion

¾ cup chopped celery

½ cup chopped green bell pepper

1¾ cups (one 14½-ounce can) stewed tomatoes, coarsely chopped
    and undrained

½ teaspoon dried minced garlic

1 tablespoon Brown Sugar Twin

16 ounces white fish, cut into 16 pieces

2 cups hot cooked rice

In a large skillet sprayed with butter-flavored cooking spray, sauté onion, celery, and green pepper for 10 minutes or until tender. Stir in undrained stewed tomatoes, garlic, and Brown Sugar Twin. Add fish. Mix gently to combine. Lower heat, cover and simmer for 20 minutes, stirring occasionally. For each serving, place ½ cup rice on a plate and spoon about 1 full cup fish mixture over top.

HINT: 1⅓ cups uncooked rice usually cooks to about 2 cups.

Each serving equals:

HE: 1¾ Vegetable • 1½ Protein • 1 Bread •
1 Optional Calorie

198 Calories • 2 gm Fat • 25 gm Protein •
20 gm Carbohydrate • 658 mg Sodium

DIABETIC: 3 Meat • 1 Vegetable • 1 Starch

Graham Cracker Caribbean Dessert

● Serves 8 (¾ cup)

1 (4-serving) package JELL-O sugar-free instant banana pudding
   mix

1 cup Carnation Nonfat Dry Milk Powder☆

1 cup (one 8-ounce can) crushed pineapple, packed in fruit juice,
   drained, and ¼ cup liquid reserved

1¼ cups water

¾ cup Yoplait plain fat-free yogurt

1 teaspoon coconut extract

Sugar substitute to equal 2 tablespoons sugar

¾ cup Cool Whip Lite

1 cup (one 11-ounce can) mandarin oranges, rinsed and drained

12 (2½-inch) graham crackers, broken into pieces

In a large bowl, combine dry pudding mix and ⅔ cup dry milk powder. Add reserved pineapple liquid and water to dry pudding mixture. Mix well using a wire whisk. In a small bowl, combine yogurt and remaining ⅓ cup dry milk powder. Stir in coconut extract, sugar substitute, and Cool Whip Lite. Add yogurt mixture to pudding mixture. Mix gently to combine. Fold in pineapple, mandarin oranges, and graham cracker pieces. Cover and refrigerate for at least 15 minutes. Gently stir again just before serving.

HINT: If not serving for at least 30 minutes, gently stir graham cracker crumbs in when serving.

Each serving equals:

HE: ½ Skim Milk • ½ Fruit • ½ Bread • ¼ Slider •
9 Optional Calories

---

146 Calories • 2 gm Fat • 5 gm Protein •
27 gm Carbohydrate • 318 mg Sodium • 0 gm Fiber

DIABETIC: 1 Starch • ½ Skim Milk • ½ Fruit *or*
2 Carbohydrate

Menu 10

Italian Tomato Mozzarella Salad
Rice and Peas Side Dish
Baked Fish Italian
Fruit Cocktail Parfait

"*Bella*" means beautiful in Italian, and what could be more "*bella*" than a meal celebrating so many delightful flavors? Here's my own quick version of that creamy Italian rice specialty, risotto, plus a delicious salad of tomatoes and mozzarella that's become an appetizer classic. No baked fish entree could be easier to prepare yet taste so romantic. Setting the stage for an evening of dancing in the moonlight (or sharing a favorite TV show on the couch) is a light and pretty dessert that'll put everyone in a great mood.

Italian Tomato Mozzarella Salad

● Serves 4 (full ⅔ cup)

> 2 cups cherry tomatoes, quartered
> 3 tablespoons (¾ ounce) shredded Kraft reduced-fat mozzarella cheese
> ¼ cup Kraft Fat Free Ranch Dressing
> 2 tablespoons Kraft Fat Free Italian Dressing
> 1 tablespoon fresh parsley or 1 teaspoon dried parsley flakes

In a medium bowl, combine tomatoes and mozzarella cheese. In a small bowl, combine Ranch dressing and Italian dressing. Pour dressing mixture over tomato mixture. Add parsley. Mix gently to combine. Cover and refrigerate for at least 15 minutes. Gently stir again just before serving.

Each serving equals:

HE: 1 Vegetable • ¼ Protein • ¼ Slider •
7 Optional Calories

57 Calories • 1 gm Fat • 2 gm Protein •
10 gm Carbohydrate • 289 mg Sodium • 1 gm Fiber

DIABETIC: 2 Vegetable

Rice and Peas Side Dish ❄

○ Serves 4 (¾ cup)

½ cup (one 2.5-ounce jar) sliced mushrooms, drained
1 (10¾-ounce) can Healthy Request Cream of Mushroom Soup
1 cup skim milk
¼ teaspoon black pepper
½ cup frozen peas
1 cup (3 ounces) uncooked instant rice
1 teaspoon dried parsley flakes

In a large skillet, combine mushrooms, mushroom soup, skim milk, and black pepper. Stir in peas. Bring mixture to a boil. Stir in rice and parsley flakes. Remove from heat, cover, and let set for 5 minutes. Stir again just before serving.

Each serving equals:

HE: 1 Bread • ¼ Vegetable • ¼ Skim Milk • ½ Slider •
1 Optional Calorie

126 Calories • 2 gm Fat • 5 gm Protein •
22 gm Carbohydrate • 433 mg Sodium • 2 gm Fiber

DIABETIC: 1½ Starch

Baked Fish Italian

● Serves 4

> 6 tablespoons (1½ ounces) dried fine bread crumbs
> 2 teaspoons Italian seasoning
> ⅓ cup Kraft Fat Free Italian Dressing
> 16 ounces white fish, cut into 4 pieces

Preheat oven to 350 degrees. Spray an 8-by-8-inch baking dish with butter-flavored cooking spray. In a sealed sandwich bag, combine bread crumbs and Italian seasoning. Pour Italian dressing into a dipping dish. Coat fish pieces in dressing, then place in sandwich bag, one piece at a time, and shake well to coat. Place fish pieces in prepared baking dish. Bake for 15 minutes or until fish flakes easily. Lightly spray tops of fish with butter-flavored cooking spray. Serve at once.

Each serving equals:

HE: 1½ Protein • ½ Bread • 5 Optional Calories

135 Calories • 3 gm Fat • 18 gm Protein •
9 gm Carbohydrate • 170 mg Sodium • 0 gm Fiber

DIABETIC: 3 Meat • ½ Starch

Fruit Cocktail Parfait

● Serves 6

⅓ cup Carnation Nonfat Dry Milk Powder

¾ cup Yoplait plain fat-free yogurt

1 (4-serving) package JELL-O sugar-free instant pistachio
pudding mix

2 cups (one 16-ounce can) fruit cocktail, packed in fruit juice,
undrained

1 cup (1 medium) diced banana

6 tablespoons Cool Whip Lite

In a medium bowl, combine dry milk powder and yogurt. Stir
in dry pudding mix. Add undrained fruit cocktail and banana. Mix
gently to combine. Evenly spoon mixture into 6 parfait or dessert
dishes. Top each with 1 tablespoon Cool Whip Lite. Refrigerate for
at least 15 minutes.

HINT: To prevent banana from turning brown, mix with 1 teaspoon lemon juice or sprinkle with Fruit Fresh.

Each serving equals:

HE: 1 Fruit • ⅓ Skim Milk • ¼ Slider •
7 Optional Calories

121 Calories • 1 gm Fat • 3 gm Protein •
25 gm Carbohydrate • 259 mg Sodium • 1 gm Fiber

DIABETIC: 1 Fruit • ½ Starch

Menu 11

Mexican Bean Salad
Adobe Vegetable Skillet
Fiesta Burgers
Hawaiian Banana Raisin Pie

Head south of the border for a fiesta of flavors that taste so delicioso your family will shout, "Olé!" Is any other cuisine as colorful or fun as Mexico's best? Now you've got a bundle of quick and healthy recipes to stir up on a moment's notice. If you love peppers and onions as much as Cliff and I do, turn up the music, set out the salsa, and enjoy! You'll still have room for a luscious piece of pie.

Mexican Bean Salad

◒ Serves 6 (⅔ cup)

> 4 cups (two 16-ounce cans) cut green beans, rinsed and drained
> ¼ cup finely chopped onion
> ¼ cup finely chopped green bell pepper
> 1½ cups frozen whole kernel corn, thawed
> ½ cup Kraft Fat Free French Dressing
> 1 teaspoon chili seasoning mix
> ¾ cup (3 ounces) shredded Kraft reduced-fat Cheddar cheese

In a large bowl, combine green beans, onion, green pepper, and corn. Add French dressing. Mix well to combine. Stir in chili seasoning mix and Cheddar cheese. Cover and refrigerate for at least 20 minutes. Gently stir again just before serving.

HINT: Thaw corn by placing in a colander and rinsing under hot water for one minute.

Each serving equals:

HE: 1½ Vegetable • ⅔ Protein • ½ Bread • 17 Optional Calories

117 Calories • 1 gm Fat • 7 gm Protein • 20 gm Carbohydrate • 359 mg Sodium • 3 gm Fiber

DIABETIC: 1 Vegetable • 1 Starch

Adobe Vegetable Skillet

◐ Serves 6 (1 cup)

1½ cups coarsely chopped onion
1½ cups coarsely chopped green bell pepper
3 full cups (16 ounces) diced cooked potatoes
2 cups chopped fresh tomatoes
¼ cup taco sauce
½ teaspoon dried minced garlic
¼ teaspoon black pepper

In a large skillet sprayed with olive oil–flavored cooking spray, sauté onion and green pepper for 5 minutes. Add potatoes. Mix well to combine. Continue cooking for another 5 minutes, stirring often. Stir in tomatoes, taco sauce, garlic, and black pepper. Lower heat and simmer for 5 minutes or until mixture is heated through, stirring often.

HINT: I left skin on both potatoes and tomatoes, but you can peel them if you prefer.

Each serving equals:

HE: 1⅔ Vegetable • ⅔ Bread

108 Calories • 0 gm Fat • 3 gm Protein • 24 gm Carbohydrate • 93 mg Sodium • 3 gm Fiber

DIABETIC: 1 Vegetable • 1 Starch

Fiesta Burgers

❂ Serves 6 (⅓ cup filling)

16 ounces ground 90% lean turkey or beef
½ cup chopped onion
½ cup chopped green bell pepper
1 (10¾-ounce) can Healthy Request Tomato Soup
2 teaspoons chili seasoning mix
¼ teaspoon black pepper
6 reduced-calorie hamburger buns

In a large skillet sprayed with olive oil–flavored cooking spray, brown meat, onion, and green pepper. Add tomato soup, chili seasoning mix, and black pepper. Mix well to combine. Lower heat and simmer for 10 minutes, stirring occasionally. Serve on hamburger buns.

Each serving equals:

HE: 2 Protein • 1 Bread • ⅓ Vegetable • ¼ Slider • 10 Optional Calories

228 Calories • 8 gm Fat • 16 gm Protein • 23 gm Carbohydrate • 425 mg Sodium • 2 gm Fiber

DIABETIC: 2 Meat • 1½ Starch

Hawaiian Banana Raisin Pie

● Serves 8

1 cup (1 medium) diced banana

1 (6-ounce) Keebler graham cracker piecrust

1 (4-serving) package JELL-O sugar-free instant banana pudding mix

⅔ cup Carnation Nonfat Dry Milk Powder

1 cup (one 8-ounce can) crushed pineapple, packed in fruit juice, drained, and ¼ cup liquid reserved

¾ cup water

1 cup Cool Whip Lite☆

½ cup raisins

1 teaspoon coconut extract

2 tablespoons flaked coconut

Layer banana in bottom of piecrust. In a medium bowl, combine dry pudding mix and dry milk powder. Add reserved pineapple liquid and water. Mix well using a wire whisk. Blend in ¼ cup Cool Whip Lite, drained pineapple, and raisins. Spread mixture evenly over bananas. Refrigerate 5 minutes. Meanwhile, in a small bowl, combine remaining ¾ cup Cool Whip Lite and coconut extract. Spread mixture evenly over set filling. Evenly sprinkle coconut over top. Refrigerate for at least 15 minutes. Cut into 8 servings.

HINTS: 1. To prevent banana from turning brown, mix with 1 teaspoon lemon juice or sprinkle with Fruit Fresh.

2. To plump up raisins without "cooking," place in a glass measuring cup and microwave on HIGH for 20 seconds.

Each serving equals:

HE: 1 Fruit • ½ Bread • ¼ Skim Milk • 1 Slider • 6 Optional Calories

230 Calories • 6 gm Fat • 4 gm Protein • 40 gm Carbohydrate • 298 mg Sodium • 2 gm Fiber

DIABETIC: 1½ Starch or Carbohydrate • 1 Fruit • 1 Fat

Menu 12

Calico Cucumber Salad
"Real Man" Gazpacho
Tex-Mex Skillet Hash
Yogurt Fruit Tarts

*Nothing tastes better on a steamy summer evening than a mug
of my tangy gazpacho! Add a fresh take on cucumber salad and
a sizzling skillet hash that's as big on flavor as Texas is big on
EVERYTHING, and you've got a meal that's as hard to forget as
the Alamo! The sweet fruit tarts take no time at all to fix but
taste so good, someone's bound to go looking for the bakery box.*

Calico Cucumber Salad

● Serves 4 (1 cup)

> 2 cups frozen whole kernel corn, thawed
> 2¾ cups unpeeled thinly sliced cucumbers
> ¼ cup finely chopped onion
> ½ cup Kraft fat-free mayonnaise
> 2 tablespoons white vinegar
> Sugar substitute to equal 1 tablespoon sugar
> ¼ teaspoon black pepper
> 1 teaspoon dried parsley flakes

In a large bowl, combine corn, cucumber, and onion. In a small
bowl, combine mayonnaise, vinegar, sugar substitute, black pepper,
and parsley flakes. Add mayonnaise mixture to vegetable mixture.

Stir gently to combine. Cover and refrigerate for at least 20 minutes. Gently stir again just before serving.

HINT: Thaw corn by placing in a colander and rinsing under hot water for one minute.

Each serving equals:

HE: 1½ Vegetable • 1 Bread • ¼ Slider •
2 Optional Calories

108 Calories • 0 gm Fat • 3 gm Protein •
24 gm Carbohydrate • 217 mg Sodium • 3 gm Fiber

DIABETIC: 1 Vegetable • 1 Starch

"Real Man" Gazpacho

○ Serves 4 (full 1 cup)

2 cups Healthy Request tomato juice or any reduced-sodium
    tomato juice
2½ cups chunky salsa (mild, medium, or hot)
1 teaspoon dried parsley flakes
¼ cup Land O Lakes no-fat sour cream

In a medium bowl, combine tomato juice, salsa, and parsley flakes. Refrigerate for at least 20 minutes. When serving, spoon mixture into mugs and top each with 1 tablespoon sour cream.

Each serving equals:

HE: 2¼ Vegetable • 15 Optional Calories

56 Calories • 0 gm Fat • 2 gm Protein •
12 gm Carbohydrate • 657 mg Sodium • 0 gm Fiber

DIABETIC: 2 Vegetable

Tex-Mex Skillet Hash ❄

○ Serves 4 (1 full cup)

> 8 ounces ground 90% lean turkey or beef
> ½ cup chopped onion
> ½ cup chopped green bell pepper
> 1¾ cups (one 15-ounce can) Hunt's Chunky Tomato Sauce
> 10 ounces (one 16-ounce can) red kidney beans, rinsed and
>   drained
> 2 teaspoons chili seasoning mix
> 1 tablespoon Brown Sugar Twin
> 1½ cups hot cooked rice

In a large skillet sprayed with olive oil–flavored cooking spray, brown meat, onion, and green pepper. Stir in tomato sauce, kidney beans, chili seasoning mix, and Brown Sugar Twin. Add rice. Mix well to combine. Lower heat and simmer for 10 minutes or until mixture is heated through, stirring occasionally.

HINT: 1 cup uncooked rice usually cooks to about 1½ cups.

Each serving equals:

HE: 2¾ Protein • 2¼ Vegetable • ¾ Bread

241 Calories • 5 gm Fat • 17 gm Protein •
32 gm Carbohydrate • 757 mg Sodium • 5 gm Fiber

DIABETIC: 2 Meat • 2 Starch • 1 Vegetable

Yogurt Fruit Tarts

● Serves 6

¾ cup Yoplait plain fat-free yogurt
⅓ cup Carnation Nonfat Dry Milk Powder
6 tablespoons apricot spreadable fruit spread
¾ cup Cool Whip Lite
¼ teaspoon almond extract
1 (6-single serve) package Keebler graham cracker crusts

In a medium bowl, combine yogurt and dry milk powder. Stir in spreadable fruit and Cool Whip Lite. Add almond extract. Mix gently to combine. Evenly spoon mixture into graham cracker crusts. Refrigerate for at least 20 minutes.

Each serving equals:

HE: 1 Fruit • ½ Bread • ⅓ Skim Milk • ¾ Slider •
10 Optional Calories

186 Calories • 6 gm Fat • 3 gm Protein •
30 gm Carbohydrate • 177 mg Sodium • 0 gm Fiber

DIABETIC: 1 Fruit • 1 Starch • 1 Fat

Menu 13

Italian Green Bean Salad
Pineapple and Orange Cottage Salad
Crunchy Loose Meat Sandwiches
Caribbean Coconut Cheesecake

Green beans are my husband Cliff's favorite vegetable, so I'm forever looking to keep him happy. This version tosses in just a few olives for fun. He's also a big fan of that Iowa favorite, loose meat sandwiches, that gives ground meat a whole new excitement—and I bet you soon will be too! With a sweet side salad and a glorious cheesecake that sings the praises of coconut, this menu offers "fast" food so flavorful and filling that even a weekday dinner will feel like a special occasion.

Italian Green Bean Salad

● Serves 8 (¾ cup)

½ cup Kraft Fat Free Italian Dressing
2 tablespoons Kraft fat-free mayonnaise
½ cup (1½ ounces) grated Kraft fat-free Parmesan cheese
6 cups (three 16-ounce cans) cut green beans, rinsed and drained
1½ cups chopped fresh tomatoes
½ cup finely chopped onion
½ cup (2 ounces) sliced ripe olives

In a large bowl, combine Italian dressing, mayonnaise, and Parmesan cheese. Stir in green beans. Add tomatoes, onion, and olives. Mix well to combine. Cover and refrigerate for at least 20 minutes. Gently stir again just before serving.

Each serving equals:
HE: 2 Vegetable • ¼ Protein • ¼ Fat •
7 Optional Calories

77 Calories • 1 gm Fat • 4 gm Protein •
13 gm Carbohydrate • 319 mg Sodium • 4 gm Fiber

DIABETIC: 2½ Vegetable

Pineapple and Orange Cottage Salad

◔ Serves 8 (¾ cup)

> 1 cup (one 11-ounce can) mandarin oranges, rinsed and drained
> 2 cups (two 8-ounce cans) crushed pineapple, packed in fruit
>   juice, drained
> 2 cups fat-free cottage cheese
> 1 (4-serving) package JELL-O sugar-free orange gelatin
> 1 cup Cool Whip Lite

In a medium bowl, combine mandarin oranges, crushed pineapple, and cottage cheese. Add dry gelatin. Mix well to combine. Blend in Cool Whip Lite. Cover and refrigerate for at least 20 minutes. Gently stir again just before serving.

Each serving equals:
HE: ¾ Fruit • ½ Protein • ¼ Slider •
5 Optional Calories

113 Calories • 1 gm Fat • 9 gm Protein •
17 gm Carbohydrate • 240 mg Sodium • 0 gm Fiber

DIABETIC: 1 Fruit • 1 Meat

Crunchy Loose Meat Sandwiches

○ Serves 8 (scant ½ cup filling)

> 16 ounces ground 90% lean turkey or beef
> ½ cup chopped onion
> 2 cups purchased coleslaw mix
> 1¾ cups (one 15-ounce can) Hunt's Chunky Tomato Sauce
> 1 teaspoon prepared mustard
> 1 teaspoon taco seasoning
> ¼ teaspoon black pepper
> 1 tablespoon Brown Sugar Twin
> 8 reduced-calorie hamburger buns

In a large skillet sprayed with butter-flavored cooking spray, brown meat and onion. Add coleslaw mix. Mix well to combine. Continue cooking for 5 minutes, stirring often. Stir in tomato sauce, mustard, taco seasoning, black pepper, and Brown Sugar Twin. Lower heat and simmer for 10 minutes, stirring occasionally. Serve on hamburger buns.

HINT: 1½ cups shredded cabbage and ½ cup shredded carrots may be used in place of purchased coleslaw mix.

Each serving equals:

HE: 1½ Protein • 1½ Vegetable • 1 Bread •
1 Optional Calorie

182 Calories • 6 gm Fat • 13 gm Protein •
19 gm Carbohydrate • 577 mg Sodium • 1 gm Fiber

DIABETIC: 1½ Meat • 1 Vegetable • 1 Starch

Caribbean Coconut Cheesecake

● Serves 8

> 2 (8-ounce) packages Philadelphia fat-free cream cheese
> 1 (4-serving) package JELL-O sugar-free instant vanilla pudding
>   mix
> ⅔ cup Carnation Nonfat Dry Milk Powder
> 1 cup water
> 1½ teaspoons coconut extract☆
> 1 teaspoon rum extract
> 1 cup Cool Whip Lite☆
> 1 (6-ounce) Keebler graham cracker piecrust
> 2 tablespoons flaked coconut

In a medium bowl, stir cream cheese with a spoon until soft. Add dry pudding mix, dry milk powder, and water. Mix well using a wire whisk. Blend in 1 teaspoon coconut extract, rum extract, and ¼ cup Cool Whip Lite. Spread mixture evenly into piecrust. Refrigerate while preparing topping. In a small bowl, combine remaining ¾ cup Cool Whip Lite and remaining ½ teaspoon coconut extract. Spread mixture evenly over filling. Evenly sprinkle coconut over top. Refrigerate for at least 20 minutes. Cut into 8 servings.

Each serving equals:

> HE: 1 Protein • ½ Bread • ¼ Skim Milk • 1 Slider •
> 6 Optional Calories
> _____
> 198 Calories • 6 gm Fat • 11 gm Protein •
> 25 gm Carbohydrate • 674 mg Sodium • 1 gm Fiber
> _____
> DIABETIC: 1½ Carbohydrate • 1 Meat • ½ Fat

Menu 14

Broccoli Fruit Slaw
Farmhouse Macaroni Bake
Saucy "Faux" Steaks
Chocolate Banana Sunset Pie

Here's a hearty cold-weather menu that's a real favorite with men. Tempt his taste buds with the sweet crunch of a coleslaw that mingles the flavors of a Waldorf salad (apples and raisins) with fresh broccoli; satisfy his growling stomach with a rich and sturdy corn pudding served alongside my saucy chopped steak. Then watch the sunset together—and relive those golden moments afterward with a piece of healthy pie!

Broccoli Fruit Slaw

◔ Serves 6 (⅔ cup)

> 3 cups purchased broccoli coleslaw mix
> 1 cup (2 small) unpeeled chopped Red Delicious apples
> 7 tablespoons raisins
> ½ cup Kraft fat-free mayonnaise
> ¼ cup unsweetened orange juice
> Sugar substitute to equal 2 tablespoons sugar

In a large bowl, combine broccoli coleslaw mix, apples, and raisins. In a small bowl, combine mayonnaise, orange juice, and sugar substitute. Add mayonnaise mixture to broccoli mixture. Mix gently to combine. Cover and refrigerate for at least 20 minutes. Gently stir again just before serving.

HINT: To plump up raisins without "cooking," place raisins in a glass measuring cup and microwave on HIGH for 20 seconds.

Each serving equals:

HE: 1 Fruit • 1 Vegetable • 15 Optional Calories

---

80 Calories • 0 gm Fat • 2 gm Protein •
18 gm Carbohydrate • 156 mg Sodium • 2 gm Fiber

DIABETIC: 1 Fruit • 1 Vegetable

Farmhouse Macaroni Bake ❄

○ Serves 6

> 1 cup hot cooked elbow macaroni, rinsed and drained
> 1 cup (one 8-ounce can) whole kernel corn, rinsed and drained
> 1 cup (one 8-ounce can) cream-style corn
> ¾ cup (3 ounces) shredded Kraft reduced-fat Cheddar cheese
> 1 teaspoon dried parsley flakes
> ¼ teaspoon black pepper
> 2 tablespoons Kraft Fat Free Catalina Dressing

Preheat oven to 350 degrees. Spray an 8-by-8-inch baking dish with butter-flavored cooking spray. In a medium bowl, combine macaroni, whole kernel corn, and cream-style corn. Stir in Cheddar cheese, parsley flakes, black pepper, and Catalina dressing. Pour mixture into prepared baking dish. Bake 25 minutes. Place baking dish on a wire rack and let set for 5 minutes. Divide into 6 servings.

HINT: ⅔ cup uncooked macaroni usually cooks to about 1 cup.

Each serving equals:

HE: 1 Bread • ⅔ Protein • 8 Optional Calories

---

134 Calories • 2 gm Fat • 7 gm Protein •
22 gm Carbohydrate • 283 mg Sodium • 1 gm Fiber

DIABETIC: 1½ Starch • ½ Meat

Saucy "Faux" Steaks

● Serves 6

16 ounces ground 90% lean turkey or beef
6 tablespoons (1½ ounces) dried fine bread crumbs
¼ cup finely chopped onion
½ cup Heinz Light Harvest or Healthy Choice ketchup☆
1¾ cups (one 14½-ounce can) stewed tomatoes, undrained

In a large bowl, combine meat, bread crumbs, onion, and ¼ cup ketchup. Mix well to combine. Using a ⅓-cup measure as a guide, form mixture into 6 patties. Place patties in a large skillet sprayed with butter-flavored cooking spray. Brown about 3 minutes on each side. In a small bowl, combine undrained stewed tomatoes and remaining ¼ cup ketchup. Pour stewed tomato mixture evenly over browned meat. Lower heat, cover, and simmer for 15 minutes. When serving, evenly spoon sauce over "steaks."

Each serving equals:

HE: 2 Protein • ⅔ Vegetable • ⅓ Bread • ½ Slider

175 Calories • 7 gm Fat • 15 gm Protein •
13 gm Carbohydrate • 467 mg Sodium • 1 gm Fiber

DIABETIC: 2 Meat • 1 Vegetable • ½ Starch

Chocolate Banana Sunset Pie

○ Serves 8

2 cups (2 medium) diced bananas

1 (6-ounce) Keebler chocolate piecrust

1 (4-serving) package JELL-O sugar-free instant chocolate
    pudding mix

⅔ cup Carnation Nonfat Dry Milk Powder

1 cup (one 8-ounce can) crushed pineapple, packed in fruit juice,
    drained, and ¼ cup liquid reserved

1 cup water

1 cup Cool Whip Lite☆

1 teaspoon coconut extract

2 tablespoons flaked coconut

1 tablespoon (¼ ounce) mini chocolate chips

Layer bananas in bottom of piecrust. In a large bowl, combine
dry pudding mix and dry milk powder. Add reserved pineapple
liquid and water. Mix well using a wire whisk. Blend in ¼ cup Cool
Whip Lite. Spread pudding mixture evenly over bananas. Refrigerate while preparing topping. In a small bowl, combine remaining
¾ cup Cool Whip Lite, coconut extract, and drained pineapple.
Spread topping mixture evenly over pudding mixture. Evenly sprinkle coconut and chocolate chips over top. Refrigerate for at least 20
minutes. Cut into 8 servings.

HINT: To prevent bananas from turning brown, mix with 1 tea-
    spoon lemon juice or sprinkle with Fruit Fresh.

Each serving equals:

HE: ¾ Fruit • ½ Bread • ¼ Skim Milk • 1 Slider •
13 Optional Calories

231 Calories • 7 gm Fat • 4 gm Protein •
38 gm Carbohydrate • 300 mg Sodium • 2 gm Fiber

DIABETIC: 1½ Starch *or* Carbohydrate • 1 Fruit • 1 Fat

Menu 15

Cauliflower Pea Salad
Easy Potato Salad
Dill Cheeseburger Meat Loaf
Summer Breeze Rice Pudding

Planning a family reunion but haven't got much time to cook? Why not stir up these favorites fast, and spend your time visiting instead of fussing over the food? These colorful salads overflow with delicious flavors, and my cheeseburger meat loaf will win you fans both young and old. You'll surely feel those sweet memories of childhood wash over you as you savor a summery rice pudding that's oh-so-sweet and good!

Cauliflower Pea Salad

○ Serves 6 (full ¾ cup)

> 2 cups chopped fresh cauliflower
> 1½ cups frozen peas, thawed
> ¾ cup chopped celery
> ¼ cup chopped onion
> ½ cup Kraft fat-free mayonnaise
> ¼ cup Kraft Fat Free Ranch Dressing
> 1 teaspoon dried parsley flakes
> Sugar substitute to equal 2 teaspoons sugar

In a large bowl, combine cauliflower, peas, celery, and onion. In a small bowl, combine mayonnaise, Ranch dressing, parsley flakes, and sugar substitute. Add dressing mixture to vegetable mixture. Mix gently to combine. Cover and refrigerate for at least 20 minutes. Gently stir again just before serving.

HINT: Thaw peas by placing in a colander and rinsing under hot water for one minute.

Each serving equals:

HE: 1 Vegetable • ½ Bread • ¼ Slider •
10 Optional Calories

72 Calories • 0 gm Fat • 3 gm Protein •
15 gm Carbohydrate • 269 mg Sodium • 3 gm Fiber

DIABETIC: 1 Vegetable • ½ Starch

Easy Potato Salad

● Serves 6 (¾ cup)

3 full cups (16 ounces) peeled and diced cooked potatoes
¾ cup finely chopped celery
¼ cup finely chopped onion
⅓ cup Kraft fat-free mayonnaise
2 teaspoons prepared mustard
1 tablespoon vinegar
Sugar substitute to equal 1 tablespoon sugar
2 tablespoons sweet pickle relish
¼ teaspoon black pepper

In a large bowl, combine potatoes, celery, and onion. In a small bowl, combine mayonnaise, mustard, vinegar, sugar substitute, pickle relish, and black pepper. Add mayonnaise mixture to potato mixture. Mix gently to combine. Cover and refrigerate for at least 20 minutes. Gently stir again just before serving.

Each serving equals:

HE: ⅔ Bread • ⅓ Vegetable • 19 Optional Calories

80 Calories • 0 gm Fat • 2 gm Protein •
18 gm Carbohydrate • 170 mg Sodium • 0 gm Fiber

DIABETIC: 1 Starch

Dill Cheeseburger Meat Loaf

● Serves 6

> 16 ounces ground 90% lean turkey or beef
> ½ cup + 1 tablespoon (2¼ ounces) dried fine bread crumbs
> ½ cup dill pickle relish
> ¾ cup (3 ounces) shredded Kraft reduced-fat Cheddar cheese
> ½ cup chopped onion
> 1 (10¾-ounce) can Healthy Request Tomato Soup☆
> 1 tablespoon Brown Sugar Twin

In a large bowl, combine meat, bread crumbs, pickle relish, Cheddar cheese, onion, and ¼ cup tomato soup. Mix well to combine. Place a small custard cup in center of deep-dish 10-inch glass pie plate or use a microwave ring mold. Evenly spread meat mixture into prepared pie plate. In a small bowl, combine remaining ¾ cup tomato soup and Brown Sugar Twin. Evenly spoon soup mixture over top of meat mixture. Microwave on HIGH (100% power) for 8 minutes. Turn dish and continue microwaving on HIGH for 8 minutes. Place baking dish on a wire rack and let set for 5 minutes. Cut into 6 servings.

Each serving equals:

HE: 2⅔ Protein • ½ Bread • ⅓ Vegetable • ¼ Slider •
11 Optional Calories

204 Calories • 8 gm Fat • 18 gm Protein •
15 gm Carbohydrate • 620 mg Sodium • 1 gm Fiber

DIABETIC: 2½ Meat • ½ Starch • ½ Vegetable

Summer Breeze Rice Pudding

○ Serves 6

1 (4-serving) package JELL-O sugar-free instant banana pudding mix
2 cups skim milk
2 cups cold cooked rice
1 cup (1 medium) diced banana
1½ cups fresh raspberries
6 tablespoons Cool Whip Lite

In a medium bowl, combine dry pudding mix and skim milk. Mix well using a wire whisk. Add rice. Mix well to combine. Gently fold in banana and raspberries. Evenly spoon mixture into 6 dessert dishes. Top each with 1 tablespoon Cool Whip Lite. Refrigerate for at least 20 minutes.

HINTS: 1. To prevent banana from turning brown, mix with 1 teaspoon lemon juice or sprinkle with Fruit Fresh.

2. 1⅓ cups uncooked rice usually cooks to about 2 cups.

Each serving equals:

HE: ⅔ Bread • ⅔ Fruit • ⅓ Skim Milk • ¼ Slider • 7 Optional Calories

145 Calories • 1 gm Fat • 4 gm Protein •
30 gm Carbohydrate • 271 mg Sodium • 2 gm Fiber

DIABETIC: 1 Starch • 1 Fruit

Menu 16

Honey Dijon Cukes
Salsa Pasta Salad
Onion Meat Loaf
Banana Boat Parfait

Don't you just love those dishes you can prepare in advance, then spoon out when everyone's in a rush to get to a softball game or club meeting? You could easily make the cukes, pasta salad, and meat loaf the day before, then whip up dessert as you warm up the meat loaf before sitting down to eat. Leftovers store easily, and I think this meat loaf tastes even better the second day!

Honey Dijon Cukes

○ Serves 4 (full ½ cup)

2½ cups unpeeled sliced cucumbers
¼ cup chopped green bell pepper
¼ cup diced onion
¼ cup Kraft Fat Free Honey Dijon Ranch Dressing
2 tablespoons Kraft fat-free mayonnaise
1 teaspoon dried parsley flakes

In a medium bowl, combine cucumbers, green pepper, and onion. In a small bowl, combine Honey Dijon Ranch dressing, mayonnaise, and parsley flakes. Add dressing mixture to cucumber mixture. Mix gently to combine. Cover and refrigerate for at least 20 minutes. Gently stir again just before serving.

Each serving equals:

HE: 1½ Vegetable • ¼ Slider • 10 Optional Calories

36 Calories • 0 gm Fat • 1 gm Protein •
8 gm Carbohydrate • 123 mg Sodium • 1 gm Fiber

DIABETIC: 1½ Vegetable

Salsa Pasta Salad

⊘ Serves 4 (full ½ cup)

⅓ cup Kraft fat-free mayonnaise
½ cup chunky salsa (mild, medium, or hot)
¼ teaspoon dried minced garlic
1 teaspoon dried parsley flakes
1½ cups cold cooked rotini pasta, rinsed and drained
½ cup frozen whole kernel corn, thawed

In a medium bowl, combine mayonnaise, salsa, garlic, and parsley flakes. Add rotini pasta and corn. Mix gently to combine. Cover and refrigerate for at least 20 minutes. Gently stir again just before serving.

HINTS: 1. 1 cup uncooked rotini pasta usually cooks to about 1½ cups.

2. Thaw corn by placing in a colander and rinsing under hot water for one minute.

Each serving equals:

HE: 1 Bread • ¼ Vegetable • 13 Optional Calories

104 Calories • 0 gm Fat • 3 gm Protein •
23 gm Carbohydrate • 251 mg Sodium • 1 gm Fiber

DIABETIC: 1½ Starch

Onion Meat Loaf

● Serves 6

> *16 ounces ground 90% lean turkey or beef*
> *6 slices reduced-calorie white bread, made into soft crumbs*
> *1 cup chopped onion*
> *1 cup (one 8-ounce can) Hunt's Tomato Sauce*☆
> *1 tablespoon Brown Sugar Twin*
> *2 teaspoons prepared mustard*
> *¼ teaspoon black pepper*

In a large bowl, combine meat, bread crumbs, onion, ⅓ cup tomato sauce, Brown Sugar Twin, mustard, and black pepper. Mix well to combine. Place a small custard cup in center of deep-dish 10-inch glass pie plate or use a microwave ring mold. Evenly spread meat mixture into prepared pie plate. Spoon remaining ⅔ cup tomato sauce evenly over top of meat mixture. Microwave on HIGH (100% power) for 8 minutes. Turn dish half turn and continue microwaving on HIGH for an additional 8 minutes. Place pie plate on a wire rack and let set for 5 minutes. Cut into 6 servings.

Each serving equals:

HE: 2 Protein • 1 Vegetable • ½ Bread •
1 Optional Calorie

170 Calories • 6 gm Fat • 17 gm Protein •
12 gm Carbohydrate • 450 mg Sodium • 0 gm Fiber

DIABETIC: 2 Meat • 1 Vegetable • ½ Starch

Banana Boat Parfait

○ Serves 4

1 (4-serving) package JELL-O sugar-free chocolate cook-and-
  serve pudding mix
⅔ cup Carnation Nonfat Dry Milk Powder
1½ cups water
1 teaspoon vanilla extract
2 cups (2 medium) diced bananas
½ cup (1 ounce) miniature marshmallows
¼ cup (1 ounce) chopped walnuts

In a medium saucepan, combine dry pudding mix, dry milk powder, and water. Cook over medium heat, stirring constantly with a wire whisk, until mixture thickens and starts to boil. Remove from heat. Stir in vanilla extract. Place saucepan on a wire rack and allow to cool for 10 minutes, stirring again after 5 minutes. Add bananas, marshmallows, and walnuts. Mix gently to combine. Evenly spoon mixture into 4 dessert dishes. Refrigerate for at least 20 minutes.

HINT: To prevent bananas from turning brown, mix with 1 teaspoon lemon juice or sprinkle with Fruit Fresh.

Each serving equals:

HE: 1 Fruit • ½ Skim Milk • ½ Fat • ¼ Protein •
¼ Slider • 18 Optional Calories

217 Calories • 5 gm Fat • 7 gm Protein •
36 gm Carbohydrate • 176 mg Sodium • 2 gm Fiber

DIABETIC: 1 Fruit • 1 Fat • 1 Starch *or*
2 Carbohydrate • 1 Fat

Menu 17

Layered Honey Dijon Tomato Salad
Garden Patch Pea Salad
Quick Turkey-'n'-Biscuits
Butter Pecan Layered Pie

Sometimes the easiest kind of cooking is just to pile one ingredient on top of another until you're done! This menu starts with a simple layered salad served up fast, adds a colorful pea dish to my healthy but traditional-tasting turkey and biscuits, then finishes with a fantasy of a layered pie that tastes too good to be "good for you"—but it is! Why not layer on those healthy ingredients instead of layering on those unwanted pounds!

Layered Honey Dijon Tomato Salad

◉ Serves 6

1½ cups shredded lettuce
3 cups chopped fresh tomatoes
¾ cup (3 ounces) shredded Kraft reduced-fat mozzarella cheese
2 teaspoons dried parsley flakes
6 tablespoons Kraft Fat Free Honey Dijon Dressing

For each serving, layer ¼ cup lettuce on salad plate, place ½ cup tomatoes over lettuce, sprinkle about 2 tablespoons mozzarella cheese and ½ teaspoon parsley flakes over tomatoes and drizzle 1 tablespoon dressing over top. Serve at once.

Each serving equals:

HE: 1½ Vegetable • ⅔ Protein • ¼ Slider •
5 Optional Calories

74 Calories • 2 gm Fat • 4 gm Protein •
10 gm Carbohydrate • 240 mg Sodium • 1 gm Fiber

DIABETIC: 2 Vegetable • ½ Meat

Garden Patch Pea Salad

● Serves 6 (⅔ cup)

2 cups frozen peas, thawed
1 cup chopped fresh tomato
¾ cup chopped celery
¼ cup finely chopped onion
¼ cup Kraft Fat Free Thousand Island Dressing
¼ cup Kraft fat-free mayonnaise
1 tablespoon fresh parsley or 1 teaspoon dried parsley flakes

In a medium bowl, combine peas, tomato, celery, and onion. In a small bowl, combine Thousand Island dressing, mayonnaise, and parsley. Add dressing mixture to vegetable mixture. Mix gently to combine. Cover and refrigerate for at least 20 minutes. Gently stir again just before serving.

HINT: Thaw peas by placing in a colander and rinsing under hot water for one minute.

Each serving equals:

HE: ⅔ Bread • ⅔ Vegetable • 15 Optional Calories

68 Calories • 0 gm Fat • 3 gm Protein •
14 gm Carbohydrate • 175 mg Sodium • 3 gm Fiber

DIABETIC: 1 Vegetable • ½ Starch

Quick Turkey-'n'-Biscuits

● Serves 6

1½ cups (8 ounces) diced cooked turkey breast
1 (10¾-ounce) can Healthy Request Cream of Chicken Soup
1 teaspoon dried onion flakes
1 teaspoon dried parsley flakes
1 cup (one 8-ounce can) sliced carrots, rinsed and drained
1 cup (one 8-ounce can) cut green beans, rinsed and drained
1 (7.5-ounce) can Pillsbury refrigerated buttermilk biscuits

Preheat oven to 400 degrees. Spray an 8-by-8-inch baking dish with butter-flavored cooking spray. In a large bowl, combine turkey, chicken soup, onion flakes, and parsley flakes. Mix well to combine. Stir in carrots and green beans. Spread turkey mixture into prepared baking dish. Separate and cut each biscuit into 4 pieces. Evenly sprinkle biscuit pieces over top of turkey mixture. Lightly spray tops of biscuit pieces with butter-flavored cooking spray. Bake for 15 minutes or until biscuits are golden brown. Place baking dish on a wire rack and let set for 2 to 3 minutes. Divide into 6 servings.

HINT: If you don't have leftovers, purchase a chunk of cooked turkey breast from your local deli.

Each serving equals:

HE: 1⅓ Protein • 1¼ Bread • ⅔ Vegetable • ¼ Slider • 10 Optional Calories

196 Calories • 4 gm Fat • 16 gm Protein • 24 gm Carbohydrate • 567 mg Sodium • 2 gm Fiber

DIABETIC: 1½ Meat • 1 Starch • 1 Vegetable

Butter Pecan Layered Pie

● Serves 8

1 (4-serving) package JELL-O sugar-free instant butterscotch
    pudding mix
⅔ cup Carnation Nonfat Dry Milk Powder
1¼ cups water
¼ cup (1 ounce) chopped pecans☆
1 (6-ounce) Keebler graham cracker piecrust
1 (8-ounce) package Philadelphia fat-free cream cheese
Sugar substitute to equal 2 tablespoons sugar
¾ cup Cool Whip Lite
1 teaspoon vanilla extract

In a large bowl, combine dry pudding mix, dry milk powder, and water. Mix well using a wire whisk. Stir in 2 tablespoons pecans. Spread mixture evenly into piecrust. Refrigerate while preparing topping. In a medium bowl, stir cream cheese with a spoon until soft. Add sugar substitute, Cool Whip Lite, and vanilla extract. Mix gently to combine. Spread topping mixture evenly over pudding mixture. Evenly sprinkle remaining 2 tablespoons pecans over top. Refrigerate for at least 20 minutes. Cut into 8 servings.

Each serving equals:

HE: ½ Bread • ½ Fat • ½ Protein • ¼ Skim Milk •
¾ Slider • 19 Optional Calories

183 Calories • 7 gm Fat • 7 gm Protein •
23 gm Carbohydrate • 506 mg Sodium • 1 gm Fiber

DIABETIC: 1½ Starch *or* Carbohydrate • 1 Fat

Menu 18

Sensational Pineapple Slaw
Creamy Green Beans and Onions
Veggie Turkey and Stuffing Skillet
Pumpkin Pudding Parfait

*Are you stumped for good ideas to use up leftover turkey the day
after Thanksgiving or Christmas? Could you eat stuffing at least
once a week? Do you dream about pumpkin pie even when it's
90 degrees outside? I've got the perfect menu to solve your
problem and feed that yearning for holiday sweets any time of
the year. This turkey skillet supper is not only delicious but
provides loads of good nutrition along with all that richly
rewarding turkey and stuffing. The pumpkin desserts will
convince your fellow diners it's definitely time to celebrate, so
invite friends and family to "gobble" together soon!*

Sensational Pineapple Slaw

○ Serves 6 (⅔ cup)

> 3 cups purchased coleslaw mix
> 1 cup (one 8-ounce can) pineapple tidbits, packed in fruit juice,
>   drained
> ⅓ cup (1½ ounces) shredded Kraft reduced-fat Cheddar cheese
> ½ cup Cool Whip Lite
> ⅓ cup Kraft fat-free mayonnaise
> 1 teaspoon lemon juice

In a medium bowl, combine coleslaw mix, pineapple, and
Cheddar cheese. In a small bowl, combine Cool Whip Lite, mayonnaise, and lemon juice. Add Cool Whip Lite mixture to coleslaw
mixture. Mix well to combine. Cover and refrigerate for at least 20
minutes. Gently stir again just before serving.

HINTS: 1. If you can't find pineapple tidbits, use pineapple
             chunks and chop coarsely.

        2. 2¼ cups shredded cabbage and ½ cup shredded car-
             rots may be used in place of purchased coleslaw mix.

Each serving equals:
HE: 1 Vegetable • ⅓ Protein • ⅓ Fruit •
18 Optional Calories

74 Calories • 2 gm Fat • 3 gm Protein •
11 gm Carbohydrate • 176 mg Sodium • 1 gm Fiber

DIABETIC: 1 Vegetable • ½ Protein • ½ Fruit

Creamy Green Beans and Onions

○ Serves 6 (⅔ cup)

> ½ cup finely chopped onion
> 1½ cups (12-fluid-ounce can) Carnation Evaporated Skim Milk
> 3 tablespoons all-purpose flour
> ¼ teaspoon lemon pepper
> 4 cups (two 16-ounce cans) cut green beans, rinsed and drained

In a large skillet sprayed with butter-flavored cooking spray, sauté onion for 5 minutes or until tender. In a covered jar, combine evaporated skim milk and flour. Shake well to blend. Pour milk mixture into skillet with onion. Add lemon pepper. Mix well to combine. Continue cooking over medium heat for 5 minutes or until mixture thickens and starts to boil, stirring often. Stir in green beans. Lower heat and simmer for 5 minutes or until mixture is heated through, stirring occasionally.

Each serving equals:
HE: 1½ Vegetable • ½ Skim Milk • 15 Optional Calories

84 Calories • 0 gm Fat • 6 gm Protein •
15 gm Carbohydrate • 75 mg Sodium • 1 gm Fiber

DIABETIC: 1½ Vegetable • ½ Skim Milk

Veggie Turkey and Stuffing Skillet

❄

○ Serves 6 (1 cup)

> 2 cups (one 16-ounce can) Healthy Request Chicken Broth
> 1 (16-ounce) package frozen carrot, broccoli, and cauliflower blend
> 1 (6-ounce) package Stove Top Chicken Flavored Stuffing Mix
> 1 (10¾-ounce) can Healthy Request Cream of Chicken Soup
> ¾ cup Yoplait plain fat-free yogurt
> ⅓ cup Carnation Nonfat Dry Milk Powder
> 1 teaspoon cornstarch
> 1½ cups (8 ounces) chopped cooked turkey breast

In a large skillet, combine chicken broth, frozen vegetables, and seasoning packet from stuffing mix. Bring mixture to a boil. Lower heat and simmer for 5 minutes. Stir in dry stuffing mix. In a small bowl, combine chicken soup, yogurt, dry milk powder, and cornstarch. Add soup mixture to stuffing mixture. Mix well to combine. Fold in turkey. Lower heat and simmer for 8 to 10 minutes, stirring occasionally.

HINTS: 1. 1 cup frozen carrots, 1 cup frozen broccoli, and 1 cup frozen cauliflower may be used in place of blended vegetables.

2. If you don't have leftovers, purchase a chunk of cooked turkey breast from your local deli.

Each serving equals:

HE: 1⅓ Protein • 1⅓ Bread • 1 Vegetable •
⅓ Skim Milk • ¼ Slider • 13 Optional Calories

267 Calories • 3 gm Fat • 21 gm Protein •
39 gm Carbohydrate • 928 mg Sodium • 2 gm Fiber

DIABETIC: 1½ Starch • 1 Meat • 1 Vegetable

Pumpkin Pudding Parfait ❄

○ Serves 6

> 1 (4-serving) package JELL-O sugar-free instant butterscotch
>   pudding mix
> ⅔ cup Carnation Nonfat Dry Milk Powder
> 1 teaspoon pumpkin pie spice
> 2 cups (one 16-ounce can) pumpkin
> 1 cup (one 8-ounce can) crushed pineapple, packed in fruit juice,
>   undrained
> ¾ cup Cool Whip Lite☆
> 2 tablespoons (½ ounce) chopped pecans

In a large bowl, combine dry pudding mix, dry milk powder, and pumpkin pie spice. Add pumpkin and undrained pineapple. Mix well using a wire whisk. Blend in ¼ cup Cool Whip Lite. Evenly spoon mixture into 6 parfait or dessert dishes. Top each with 1 tablespoon Cool Whip Lite and 1 teaspoon pecans. Refrigerate for at least 20 minutes.

Each serving equals:

HE: ⅔ Vegetable • ⅓ Fruit • ⅓ Skim Milk • ⅓ Fat •
¼ Slider • 15 Optional Calories

146 Calories • 2 gm Fat • 4 gm Protein •
28 gm Carbohydrate • 273 mg Sodium • 3 gm Fiber

DIABETIC: 1 Starch • 1 Fruit

Menu 19

Viva la Carrot Salad
Thai Vegetable Pasta Salad
Easy Glazed Chicken
Layered Chocolate Raspberry Pie

Did you think you'd never again get to enjoy the decadent and delightful taste of peanut butter, now that you're eating healthy? If you feared the worst, I've got good news—you can enjoy just about any taste you like in moderation, especially when it's part of a Healthy Exchanges recipe like Thai Vegetable Pasta Salad. You'll smile as you crunch those peanuts and bite into delicious pea pods and peppers, then grin even wider when you realize this dish is just one of the pleasures of this meal. My glazed chicken cooks up pretty enough for company, and the pie that follows will remind your guests of the best chocolate raspberry truffles you can buy!

Viva la Carrot Salad

○ Serves 4 (full ½ cup)

2 cups shredded carrots
½ cup diced onion
¼ cup Kraft Fat Free French Dressing
1 teaspoon dried parsley flakes
2 tablespoons Kraft fat-free mayonnaise

In a medium bowl, combine carrots and onion. Add French dressing, parsley flakes, and mayonnaise. Mix gently to combine. Cover and refrigerate for at least 20 minutes. Gently stir again just before serving.

Each serving equals:

HE: 1¼ Vegetable • ¼ Slider • 2 Optional Calories

52 Calories • 0 gm Fat • 1 gm Protein •
12 gm Carbohydrate • 193 mg Sodium • 2 gm Fiber

DIABETIC: 2 Vegetable

Thai Vegetable Pasta Salad

○ Serves 4 (¾ cup)

2 cups cold cooked rotini pasta, rinsed and drained
1½ cups fresh pea pods
¼ cup chopped red or green bell pepper
¼ cup sliced green onion
¼ cup (1 ounce) chopped dry-roasted peanuts
3 tablespoons Kraft fat-free mayonnaise
2 tablespoons reduced-sodium soy sauce
2 tablespoons lemon juice
Sugar substitute to equal 1 tablespoon sugar
2 tablespoons Peter Pan reduced-fat peanut butter

In a large bowl, combine rotini pasta, pea pods, red or green pepper, onion, and peanuts. In a medium bowl, combine mayonnaise, soy sauce, lemon juice, sugar substitute, and peanut butter. Mix well until smooth, using a wire whisk. Add mayonnaise mixture to pasta mixture. Mix gently to combine. Cover and refrigerate for at least 20 minutes. Gently stir again just before serving.

HINT: 1½ cups uncooked rotini pasta usually cooks to about 2 cups.

Each serving equals:

HE: 1 Bread • 1 Vegetable • 1 Fat • ¾ Protein •
9 Optional Calories

231 Calories • 7 gm Fat • 9 gm Protein •
33 gm Carbohydrate • 139 mg Sodium • 3 gm Fiber

DIABETIC: 1½ Starch • 1 Vegetable • 1 Fat • ½ Meat

Easy Glazed Chicken

○ Serves 4

> 16 ounces skinned and boned uncooked chicken breast, cut into 4
>   pieces
> 1 tablespoon dried onion flakes
> ¼ cup Kraft Fat Free French Dressing
> ¼ cup apricot spreadable fruit spread
> 2 tablespoons water
> 1 teaspoon dried parsley flakes

In a large skillet sprayed with butter-flavored cooking spray, brown chicken pieces for 3 minutes on each side. In a small bowl, combine onion flakes, French dressing, fruit spread, water, and parsley flakes. Spoon dressing mixture evenly over chicken pieces. Lower heat, cover, and simmer for 15 minutes or until chicken is tender. When serving, evenly spoon sauce over chicken pieces.

Each serving equals:

HE: 3 Protein • 1 Fruit • ¼ Slider • 5 Optional Calories

244 Calories • 4 gm Fat • 35 gm Protein •
17 gm Carbohydrate • 219 mg Sodium • 0 gm Fiber

DIABETIC: 3 Meat • 1 Fruit

Layered Chocolate Raspberry Pie

● Serves 8

> 2 (4-serving) packages JELL-O sugar-free instant chocolate
>   pudding mix
> 1 (4-serving) package JELL-O sugar-free raspberry gelatin
> 1⅓ cups Carnation Nonfat Dry Milk Powder
> 2½ cups water
> 1 (6-ounce) Keebler chocolate piecrust
> ½ cup raspberry spreadable fruit spread
> ¾ cup Cool Whip Lite

In a large bowl, combine dry pudding mixes, dry gelatin, dry milk powder, and water. Mix well using a wire whisk. Spread pudding mixture evenly into piecrust. Refrigerate 5 minutes. Evenly spread spreadable fruit over pudding mixture. Spread Cool Whip Lite evenly over top. Refrigerate for at least 20 minutes. Cut into 8 servings.

HINTS: 1.   Spreadable fruit spreads best at room temperature.

          2.   Any compatible gelatin and spreadable fruit combination may be used.

Each serving equals:

HE: 1 Fruit • ½ Bread • ½ Skim Milk • 1 Slider •
19 Optional Calories

238 Calories • 6 gm Fat • 6 gm Protein •
40 gm Carbohydrate • 369 mg Sodium • 1 gm Fiber

DIABETIC: 1½ Starch • 1 Fruit • 1 Fat

Menu 20

Golden Broccoli Salad
French Quarter Carrots
Mex-Italian Chicken Skillet
Grape Cream Pie

One of the challenges I face every day is finding innovative ways to prepare vegetables. When you're bored, that's when you're most apt to go looking for high-fat goodies that last a moment on the lips, then settle in for a lifetime on the hips! Instead, why not enjoy a broccoli salad that mingles bits of bacon and cheese with those healthy veggies, then treat your family to my New Orleans–style carrots served piping hot? When their appetites are really whetted, serve a speedy skillet that's so tangy and spicy you won't be sure whether you're in Acapulco or Venice! If you've still got room for dessert, this one's a true delight.

Golden Broccoli Salad

● Serves 4 (1 cup)

3 cups chopped fresh broccoli
¾ cup shredded carrots
¼ cup chopped onion
⅓ cup (1½ ounces) shredded Kraft reduced-fat Cheddar cheese
2 tablespoons Hormel Bacon Bits
⅔ cup Kraft fat-free mayonnaise
Sugar substitute to equal 2 tablespoons sugar
1½ teaspoons prepared mustard
2 tablespoons skim milk

In a large bowl, combine broccoli, carrots, onion, Cheddar cheese, and bacon bits. In a small bowl, combine mayonnaise, sugar substitute, mustard, and skim milk. Add mayonnaise mixture to broccoli mixture. Mix gently to combine. Cover and refrigerate for at least 20 minutes. Gently stir again just before serving.

Each serving equals:

HE: 2 Vegetable • ½ Protein • ½ Slider •
5 Optional Calories

---

115 Calories • 3 gm Fat • 7 gm Protein •
15 gm Carbohydrate • 482 mg Sodium • 3 gm Fiber

DIABETIC: 2 Vegetable • ½ Meat

French Quarter Carrots

○ Serves 4 (full ⅔ cup)

4 cups shredded carrots	2 tablespoons Brown Sugar
½ cup chopped onion	Twin
½ cup chopped green bell	1 teaspoon prepared mustard
pepper	1 teaspoon dried parsley flakes
½ cup water	⅛ teaspoon black pepper

In a large skillet sprayed with butter-flavored cooking spray, sauté carrots, onion, and green pepper for 5 minutes, stirring often. Add water. Mix well to combine. Lower heat, cover and simmer for 10 minutes or until vegetables are tender and most of the liquid is evaporated, stirring occasionally. Stir in Brown Sugar Twin, mustard, parsley flakes, and black pepper. Continue cooking for 2 to 3 minutes, stirring often.

Each serving equals:

HE: 2½ Vegetable • 3 Optional Calories

---

56 Calories • 0 gm Fat • 1 gm Protein •
13 gm Carbohydrate • 46 mg Sodium • 2 gm Fiber

DIABETIC: 2 Vegetable

Mex-Italian Chicken Skillet

○ Serves 4 (1 cup)

> 3 tablespoons all-purpose flour
> 1 teaspoon Italian seasoning
> 16 ounces skinned and boned uncooked chicken breast, cut into
>   24 pieces
> 2 tablespoons skim milk
> 1¾ cups (one 15-ounce can) Hunt's Chunky Tomato Sauce
> ½ cup chunky salsa (mild, medium, or hot)
> 1½ cups hot cooked spaghetti, rinsed and drained
> ¼ cup (¾ ounce) grated Kraft fat-free Parmesan cheese

In a saucer, combine flour and Italian seasoning. Dip chicken pieces in skim milk, then into flour mixture. (Reserve any remaining flour.) Place chicken pieces in a large skillet sprayed with olive oil–flavored cooking spray. Brown chicken pieces for 4 minutes, stirring often. In a medium bowl, combine tomato sauce, salsa, and any remaining flour mixture. Add sauce mixture. Mix well to combine. Lower heat, cover and simmer for 10 minutes, stirring occasionally. Stir in spaghetti and Parmesan cheese. Continue cooking for 5 minutes or until mixture is heated through, stirring often.

HINT: Full 1 cup uncooked spaghetti usually cooks to about 1½ cups.

Each serving equals:

HE: 3¼ Protein • 2 Vegetable • 1 Bread •
3 Optional Calories

292 Calories • 4 gm Fat • 36 gm Protein •
28 gm Carbohydrate • 968 mg Sodium • 2 gm Fiber

DIABETIC: 3 Meat • 2 Vegetable • 1 Starch

Grape Cream Pie

○ Serves 8

> 1 (4-serving) package JELL-O sugar-free instant vanilla pudding mix
>
> ⅔ cup Carnation Nonfat Dry Milk Powder
>
> 1¼ cups Diet Rite white grape soda or water
>
> 1 cup (6 ounces) Thompson grapes, sliced
>
> 1 (6-ounce) Keebler shortbread piecrust
>
> ¾ cup Cool Whip Lite
>
> ½ teaspoon coconut extract
>
> 2 tablespoons flaked coconut

In a medium bowl, combine dry pudding mix, dry milk powder, and Diet Rite soda. Mix well using a wire whisk. Stir in grapes. Spread mixture evenly into piecrust. Refrigerate while preparing topping. In a small bowl, combine Cool Whip Lite and coconut extract. Spread topping mixture evenly over pudding mixture. Evenly sprinkle coconut over top. Refrigerate for at least 20 minutes. Cut into 8 servings.

Each serving equals:

HE: ½ Bread • ¼ Fruit • ¼ Skim Milk • 1 Slider •
2 Optional Calories

170 Calories • 6 gm Fat • 3 gm Protein •
26 gm Carbohydrate • 300 mg Sodium • 1 gm Fiber

DIABETIC: 1½ Carbohydrate • 1 Fat

Menu 21

Dilly Veggie Salad
Blushing Cauliflower
Quickie Chicken Rice Skillet
Warm Apple Banana Ice Cream Treats

Are you expecting to leave the table feeling hungry because you've chosen a healthy lifestyle? Well, with my Healthy Exchanges menus you're more likely to find yourself "almost" too stuffed for dessert! Here's more of the great-tasting food I've created to satisfy and surprise you, from a rainbow salad to a cauliflower and cheese combo that smells too good to believe, from a delectably creamy chicken and rice entree to some quick and easy ice cream treats that will make folks of any age feel like kids again!

Dilly Veggie Salad

○ Serves 4 (1 cup)

1½ cups thinly sliced carrots
1¼ cups unpeeled chopped cucumbers
¾ cup thinly sliced radishes
1 cup chopped fresh broccoli
½ cup Kraft Fat Free Ranch Dressing
¼ cup Kraft fat-free mayonnaise
½ teaspoon dried dill weed

In a medium bowl, combine carrots, cucumbers, radishes, and broccoli. In a small bowl, combine Ranch dressing, mayonnaise, and dill weed. Add dressing mixture to vegetable mixture. Mix gently to combine. Cover and refrigerate for at least 20 minutes. Gently stir again just before serving.

Each serving equals:

HE: 2¼ Vegetable • ¾ Slider • 15 Optional Calories

88 Calories • 0 gm Fat • 1 gm Protein • 21 gm Carbohydrate • 389 mg Sodium • 2 gm Fiber

DIABETIC: 2 Vegetable • ½ Starch

Blushing Cauliflower

◎ Serves 4 (¾ cup)

3 cups frozen cut cauliflower
1½ cups water
1 (10¾-ounce) can Healthy Request Tomato Soup
½ teaspoon dried minced garlic
2 teaspoons dried parsley flakes
1 teaspoon prepared mustard
¼ teaspoon lemon pepper
⅓ cup (1½ ounces) shredded Kraft reduced-fat Cheddar cheese

In a medium saucepan, cook cauliflower in water for 10 minutes or just until tender. Drain. In a large skillet, combine tomato soup, garlic, parsley flakes, mustard, and lemon pepper. Add Cheddar cheese. Mix well to combine. Stir in cauliflower. Lower heat and simmer for 5 minutes or until cheese melts, stirring often.

Each serving equals:

HE: 1½ Vegetable • ½ Protein • ½ Slider • 5 Optional Calories

111 Calories • 3 gm Fat • 5 gm Protein • 16 gm Carbohydrate • 453 mg Sodium • 5 gm Fiber

DIABETIC: 1½ Vegetable • ½ Starch

Quickie Chicken Rice Skillet ❄

○ Serves 4 (1 full cup)

1 (10¾-ounce) can Healthy Request Cream of Chicken Soup
1 cup skim milk
2 teaspoons reduced-sodium soy sauce
1½ cups (8 ounces) diced cooked chicken breast
½ cup frozen peas
¼ cup canned chopped pimientos
¼ teaspoon black pepper
1 cup (3 ounces) uncooked instant rice

In a large skillet, combine chicken soup, skim milk, and soy sauce. Stir in chicken, peas, pimientos, and black pepper. Bring mixture to a boil. Add rice. Mix well to combine. Remove from heat, cover, and let set for 5 minutes. Stir again just before serving.

HINT: If you don't have leftovers, purchase a chunk of cooked chicken breast from your local deli.

Each serving equals:

HE: 2 Protein • 1 Bread • ¼ Skim Milk • ½ Slider •
5 Optional Calories

216 Calories • 4 gm Fat • 23 gm Protein •
22 gm Carbohydrate • 414 mg Sodium • 1 gm Fiber

DIABETIC: 2 Meat • 2 Starch

Warm Apple Banana Ice Cream Treats

● Serves 4

1 cup (1 medium) sliced banana
1 cup (2 small) cored, unpeeled, and diced cooking apples
¼ cup apricot spreadable fruit spread
2 tablespoons (½ ounce) chopped pecans
1 cup Wells' Blue Bunny sugar-free and fat-free vanilla ice cream
  or any sugar- and fat-free ice cream

Evenly divide banana and apples among four (6-ounce) custard cups. Spoon 1 tablespoon fruit spread and 1½ teaspoons pecans over top of each. Microwave on HIGH (100% power) for 2 to 3 minutes or until hot. Top each with ¼ cup ice cream. Serve at once.

Each serving equals:

HE: 2 Fruit • ¼ Fat • ¼ Slider • 5 Optional Calories

146 Calories • 2 gm Fat • 2 gm Protein •
30 gm Carbohydrate • 40 mg Sodium • 1 gm Fiber

DIABETIC: 2 Fruit • ½ Fat

Menu 22

Riviera Salad
Tomato Patch Chicken Rice Soup
Grilled Cheese and Ham Sandwich
Tropical Pleasure Pie

Who says a soup and sandwich supper has to be ordinary? Not when the chef has a few Healthy Exchanges tricks under her hat! Try this soothing chunky soup so full of chicken and rice, you'll wonder if you're eating a satisfying stew. Add a luscious fresh salad that stirs up in an instant, the perfect grilled-cheese sandwich, and a dessert that tastes like you hopped a jet to the islands without leaving your table! Isn't it great that you can treat yourself well and feed your family in a healthy way without giving up the foods and flavors that make you feel happy?

Riviera Salad

● Serves 4 (1 cup)

2 cups unpeeled thinly sliced cucumbers
1½ cups chopped fresh tomato
½ cup finely chopped celery
½ cup Kraft Fat Free French Dressing
1 tablespoon fresh parsley or 1 teaspoon dried parsley flakes

In a medium bowl, combine cucumbers, tomato, and celery. Add French dressing and parsley. Mix gently to combine. Cover and refrigerate for at least 20 minutes. Gently stir again just before serving.

Each serving equals:
HE: 2 Vegetable • ½ Slider

56 Calories • 0 gm Fat • 1 gm Protein •
13 gm Carbohydrate • 261 mg Sodium • 1 gm Fiber

DIABETIC: 2 Vegetable

Tomato Patch Chicken Rice Soup

● Serves 4 (1½ cups)

1 full cup (6 ounces) diced cooked chicken breast
2 cups (one 16-ounce can) Healthy Request Chicken Broth
2 cups water
1¾ cups (one 15-ounce can) Hunt's Chunky Tomato Sauce
1 cup (3 ounces) uncooked instant rice
1 teaspoon dried parsley flakes
¼ teaspoon black pepper

In a large saucepan, combine chicken breast, chicken broth, water, and tomato sauce. Bring mixture to a boil. Lower heat and simmer for 5 minutes. Stir in rice, parsley flakes, and black pepper. Remove from heat, cover, and let set for 5 minutes. Stir again just before serving.

HINT: If you don't have leftovers, purchase a chunk of cooked chicken breast from your local deli.

Each serving equals:
HE: 1¾ Vegetable • 1½ Protein • ¾ Bread •
16 Optional Calories

105 Calories • 1 gm Fat • 16 gm Protein •
8 gm Carbohydrate • 340 mg Sodium • 0 gm Fiber

DIABETIC: 1½ Meat • 1 Vegetable • ½ Starch

Grilled Cheese and Ham Sandwich

● Serves 4

¼ cup Kraft fat-free mayonnaise
1 teaspoon prepared mustard
8 slices reduced-calorie white bread
1 (6-ounce) package Healthy Choice sliced 97% fat-free ham
4 (¾-ounce) slices Kraft reduced-fat American cheese

Spray a large skillet with butter-flavored cooking spray. In a small bowl, combine mayonnaise and mustard. Spread mayonnaise mixture evenly over 4 slices of bread. Evenly divide and layer ham slices over top and arrange 1 slice American cheese and remaining slices of bread on top of each. Place sandwiches in skillet. Cover and brown on medium heat, for about 3 minutes. Lightly spray tops of bread with butter-flavored cooking spray and flip sandwiches over. Cover skillet again and brown just until cheese is melted, about 1 to 2 minutes. Serve at once.

HINT: Bread browns quickly, so watch closely.

Each serving equals:

HE: 2 Protein • 1 Bread • 10 Optional Calories

167 Calories • 3 gm Fat • 17 gm Protein •
18 gm Carbohydrate • 747 mg Sodium • 0 gm Fiber

DIABETIC: 2 Meat • 1 Starch

Tropical Pleasure Pie

● Serves 8

    1 cup (1 medium) diced banana

    1 (6-ounce) Keebler graham cracker piecrust

    1 (4-serving) package JELL-O sugar-free instant pistachio
        pudding mix

    ⅔ cup Carnation Nonfat Dry Milk Powder

    1 cup (one 8-ounce can) crushed pineapple, packed in fruit juice,
        drained, and ¼ cup liquid reserved

    1 cup water

    1 cup Cool Whip Lite☆

    1 cup (one 11-ounce can) mandarin oranges, rinsed and drained

    1 teaspoon coconut extract

    2 tablespoons flaked coconut

Layer banana in bottom of piecrust. In a large bowl, combine dry pudding mix and dry milk powder. Add reserved pineapple liquid and water. Mix well using a wire whisk. Blend in ¼ cup Cool Whip Lite. Add pineapple and mandarin oranges. Mix gently to combine. Spread mixture evenly over banana. Refrigerate while preparing topping. In a small bowl, combine remaining ¾ cup Cool Whip Lite and coconut extract. Spread topping mixture evenly over pudding mixture. Evenly sprinkle coconut over top. Refrigerate for at least 20 minutes. Cut into 8 servings.

HINT: To prevent banana from turning brown, mix with 1 teaspoon lemon juice or sprinkle with Fruit Fresh.

Each serving equals:

    HE: ¾ Fruit • ½ Bread • ¼ Skim Milk • 1 Slider •
    6 Optional Calories

---

    206 Calories • 6 gm Fat • 3 gm Protein •
    35 gm Carbohydrate • 331 mg Sodium • 1 gm Fiber

    DIABETIC: 1 Fruit • 1 Starch • 1 Fat

Menu 23

Easy Coleslaw
Green Beans and Pimiento Salad
Creamy Chicken and Vegetable Skillet
Hawaiian Pudding Dessert

My husband and kids wouldn't mind if we had coleslaw nearly every day—how about yours? This creamy version is one of our favorites, perfect for days when you haven't got much time to cook but long for a great-tasting meal anyway. This entire menu delivers so much creamy goodness, you can't help but wonder how such yummy food can be healthy—creamy green beans and onions, a smooth and scrumptious chicken and veggie skillet, and a delectable pineapple dessert full of goodies like coconut, pecans, and cherries. "Impossibly delicious," your family will say, but you've made the impossible happen!

Easy Coleslaw

⊙ Serves 4 (¾ cup)

> 6 tablespoons Land O Lakes no-fat sour cream
> 2 tablespoons white vinegar
> Sugar substitute to equal ¼ cup sugar
> ½ teaspoon lemon pepper
> ½ teaspoon prepared mustard
> 4 cups finely shredded cabbage

In a large bowl, combine sour cream, vinegar, sugar substitute, lemon pepper, and mustard. Add cabbage. Mix well to combine. Cover and refrigerate for at least 20 minutes. Gently stir again just before serving.

Each serving equals:

HE: 2 Vegetable • ¼ Slider • 9 Optional Calories

48 Calories • 0 gm Fat • 2 gm Protein •
10 gm Carbohydrate • 54 mg Sodium • 1 gm Fiber

DIABETIC: 2 Vegetable

Green Beans and Pimiento Salad

○ Serves 4 (full ½ cup)

> 2 cups (one 16-ounce can) cut green beans, rinsed and drained
> ¼ cup finely chopped onion
> ¼ cup canned sliced pimientos
> 2 tablespoons Land O Lakes no-fat sour cream
> ¼ cup Kraft fat-free mayonnaise
> 1 tablespoon skim milk
> Sugar substitute to equal 2 teaspoons sugar
> ¼ teaspoon black pepper

In a medium bowl, combine green beans, onion, and pimientos. In a small bowl, combine sour cream, mayonnaise, skim milk, sugar substitute, and black pepper. Add sour cream mixture to green bean mixture. Mix gently to combine. Cover and refrigerate for at least 20 minutes. Gently stir again just before serving.

Each serving equals:

HE: 1¼ Vegetable • ¼ Slider

40 Calories • 0 gm Fat • 2 gm Protein •
8 gm Carbohydrate • 121 mg Sodium • 1 gm Fiber

DIABETIC: 1 Vegetable

Creamy Chicken and Vegetable Skillet

◦ Serves 4 (1 cup)

3½ cups purchased stir-fry vegetables (fresh or frozen)
⅓ cup water
1 full cup (6 ounces) diced cooked chicken breast
1 (10¾-ounce) can Healthy Request Cream of Chicken Soup
¼ teaspoon black pepper

In a large skillet sprayed with butter-flavored cooking spray, sauté vegetables for 5 minutes, stirring often. Stir in water. Lower heat, cover, and simmer 5 minutes. Add chicken, chicken soup, and black pepper. Mix well to combine. Continue cooking for 5 minutes or until mixture is heated through, stirring occasionally.

HINTS: 1. If you don't want to use purchased stir-fry vegetables, use any vegetable combination of your choice.

2. If you don't have leftovers, purchase a chunk of cooked chicken breast from your local deli.

Each serving equals:

HE: 1¾ Vegetable • 1½ Protein • ½ Slider •
5 Optional Calories

142 Calories • 2 gm Fat • 13 gm Protein •
18 gm Carbohydrate • 396 mg Sodium • 3 gm Fiber

DIABETIC: 2 Vegetable • 1½ Meat • ½ Starch

Hawaiian Pudding Dessert

● Serves 8

12 (2½-inch) graham cracker squares☆
1 (4-serving) package JELL-O sugar-free instant vanilla pudding mix
⅔ cup Carnation Nonfat Dry Milk Powder
1 cup (one 8-ounce can) crushed pineapple, packed in fruit juice, undrained

½ cup water
1 cup (1 medium) diced banana
1 cup Cool Whip Lite
1 teaspoon coconut extract
2 tablespoons (½ ounce) chopped pecans
2 tablespoons flaked coconut
4 maraschino cherries, halved

Evenly arrange 9 of the graham crackers in a 9-by-9-inch cake pan. In a large bowl, combine dry pudding mix, dry milk powder, undrained pineapple, and water. Mix well using a wire whisk. Fold in banana. Evenly spread mixture over graham crackers. In a small bowl, combine Cool Whip Lite and coconut extract. Spread topping mixture evenly over pudding mixture. Crush remaining 3 graham crackers. In a small bowl, combine cracker crumbs, pecans, and coconut. Evenly sprinkle crumb mixture over top. Garnish with cherry halves. Refrigerate for at least 20 minutes. Cut into 8 servings.

HINT: To prevent banana from turning brown, mix with 1 teaspoon lemon juice or sprinkle with Fruit Fresh.

Each serving equals:

HE: ½ Bread • ½ Fruit • ¼ Skim Milk • ¼ Fat • ½ Slider • 1 Optional Calorie

147 Calories • 3 gm Fat • 3 gm Protein • 27 gm Carbohydrate • 267 mg Sodium • 1 gm Fiber

DIABETIC: 1 Starch • 1 Fat • ½ Fruit

Menu 24

Cabbage Angel Salad
Grandma's "Baked" Beans
BBQ Ham-Macaroni Salad
Apricot-Pecan Tarts

Here's a buffet that's perfect for family get-togethers or anytime you want a meal that's fun to eat, fast to prepare, and always turns out perfectly! This salad blends some unusual ingredients (trust me!) but once you try it, see if you don't think it's a piece of heaven on a plate. My simple baked beans are surprisingly good, especially when offered alongside a ham and macaroni salad that stirs up fast and full of flavor. Keep some tart shells in your pantry, and whenever you feel like a fancy-looking dessert that takes seconds to whip up, pull out this recipe. You can vary the taste by choosing your favorite spreadable fruit.

Cabbage Angel Salad

○ Serves 6 (full ½ cup)

> 3 cups shredded cabbage
> ½ cup (1 ounce) miniature marshmallows
> 1 cup (1 medium) diced banana
> 1 cup (one 8-ounce can) crushed pineapple, packed in fruit juice,
>   undrained
> ⅓ cup Kraft fat-free mayonnaise

In a medium bowl, combine cabbage, marshmallows, and banana. In a small bowl, combine undrained pineapple and mayonnaise. Add pineapple mixture to cabbage mixture. Mix well to combine. Cover and refrigerate for at least 20 minutes. Gently stir again just before serving.

HINT: To prevent banana from turning brown, mix with 1 teaspoon lemon juice or sprinkle with Fruit Fresh.

Each serving equals:

HE: 1 Vegetable • ⅔ Fruit • 17 Optional Calories

80 Calories • 0 gm Fat • 1 gm Protein •
19 gm Carbohydrate • 101 mg Sodium • 1 gm Fiber

DIABETIC: 1 Fruit • 1 Free Vegetable

Grandma's "Baked" Beans ❄

◑ Serves 6 (full ¾ cup)

1 cup finely chopped onion
½ cup finely chopped green bell pepper
2 tablespoons Hormel Bacon Bits
20 ounces (two 16-ounce cans) great northern beans, rinsed and
*   drained*
1¾ cups (one 15-ounce can) Hunt's Chunky Tomato Sauce
1 tablespoon Brown Sugar Twin
¼ teaspoon black pepper

In a large skillet sprayed with butter-flavored cooking spray, sauté onion, green pepper, and bacon bits for 5 minutes or until vegetables are tender. Add great northern beans, tomato sauce, Brown Sugar Twin, and black pepper. Mix well to combine. Lower heat and simmer for 20 minutes, stirring occasionally.

Each serving equals:

HE: 1⅔ Protein • 1⅔ Vegetable • 9 Optional Calories

141 Calories • 1 gm Fat • 9 gm Protein •
24 gm Carbohydrate • 101 mg Sodium • 6 gm Fiber

DIABETIC: 1 Starch • 1 Vegetable • 1 Meat

BBQ Ham-Macaroni Salad

○ Serves 6 (⅔ cup)

> 2 cups cold cooked elbow macaroni, rinsed and drained
> 1 cup frozen peas, thawed
> 1 full cup (6 ounces) diced Dubuque 97% fat-free ham or any
>   extra-lean ham
> ½ cup Kraft fat-free mayonnaise
> 3 tablespoons Healthy Choice BBQ sauce
> 1 teaspoon dried parsley flakes

In a large bowl, combine macaroni, peas, and ham. In a small bowl, combine mayonnaise, BBQ sauce, and parsley flakes. Add mayonnaise mixture to macaroni mixture. Mix gently to combine. Cover and refrigerate for at least 20 minutes. Gently stir again just before serving.

HINTS: 1.   1⅓ cups uncooked macaroni usually cooks to about 2 cups.

2.   To thaw peas, place in a colander and rinse under hot water for one minute.

Each serving equals:

HE: 1 Bread • ⅔ Protein • ¼ Slider • 3 Optional Calories

129 Calories • 1 gm Fat • 8 gm Protein •
22 gm Carbohydrate • 498 mg Sodium • 2 gm Fiber

DIABETIC: 1½ Starch • ½ Meat

Apricot-Pecan Tarts

○ Serves 6

1 (4-serving) package JELL-O sugar-free instant vanilla pudding
   mix
⅔ cup Carnation Nonfat Dry Milk Powder
1⅓ cups water
6 tablespoons apricot spreadable fruit spread
3 tablespoons (¾ ounce) chopped pecans
1 (6-single serve) package Keebler graham cracker crusts
6 tablespoons Cool Whip Lite

In a medium bowl, combine dry pudding mix, dry milk powder, and water. Mix well using a wire whisk. Blend in apricot spreadable fruit and pecans. Evenly spoon mixture into crusts. Top each with 1 tablespoon Cool Whip Lite. Refrigerate for at least 20 minutes.

Each serving equals:

HE: 1 Fruit • ¾ Fat • ½ Bread • ⅓ Skim Milk •
¾ Slider • 17 Optional Calories

240 Calories • 8 gm Fat • 4 gm Protein •
38 gm Carbohydrate • 456 mg Sodium • 1 gm Fiber

DIABETIC: 1½ Starch • 1 Fat *or*
1½ Carbohydrate • 1 Fat • 1 Fruit

Menu 25

Tropical Waldorf Salad
Schnitzel Carrots
Macaroni-Ham Skillet
Cherry Cola Cheesecake

I like to take a good thing and make it even better, whisking out the extra fat and sugar, and whisking in extra flavor. In this Waldorf salad, it's the bananas and coconut that get your attention; in this saucy tomato-carrot dish, it's bits of real bacon; in the skillet entree, it's the blend of two reduced-fat cheeses that add up to an even better taste than either one alone; and in this unusual cheesecake, it's the unexpected blend of cherry and cola! Don't you just love surprises that taste this special?

Tropical Waldorf Salad

● Serves 6 (½ cup)

1 cup (1 medium) diced banana
¼ cup raisins
1 cup (2 small) cored, unpeeled, and diced Red Delicious apples
1 cup diced celery
½ cup (1 ounce) miniature marshmallows
2 tablespoons (½ ounce) chopped pecans
½ cup Kraft fat-free mayonnaise
1 teaspoon lemon juice
2 teaspoons Brown Sugar Twin
½ teaspoon coconut extract
2 tablespoons flaked coconut

In a medium bowl, combine banana, raisins, apples, celery, marshmallows, and pecans. In a small bowl, combine mayonnaise, lemon juice, Brown Sugar Twin, and coconut extract. Add mayonnaise mixture to banana mixture. Mix gently to combine. Cover and refrigerate for at least 20 minutes. Gently stir again just before serving. When serving, sprinkle 1 teaspoon coconut over top of each.

HINTS: 1.   To prevent banana from turning brown, mix with 1 teaspoon lemon juice or sprinkle with Fruit Fresh.

         2.   To plump up raisins without "cooking," place in a glass measuring cup and microwave on HIGH for 20 seconds.

Each serving equals:

HE: 1 Fruit • ⅓ Vegetable • ⅓ Fat • ¼ Slider • 7 Optional Calories

110 Calories • 2 gm Fat • 1 gm Protein • 22 gm Carbohydrate • 166 mg Sodium • 2 gm Fiber

DIABETIC: 1½ Fruit • ½ Fat

Schnitzel Carrots

● Serves 6 (1 cup)

> ½ cup finely chopped onion
> 1¾ cups (one 15-ounce can) Hunt's Chunky Tomato Sauce
> ¼ cup water
> ¼ teaspoon lemon pepper
> 2 tablespoons Brown Sugar Twin
> 1 tablespoon Sugar Twin or Sprinkle Sweet
> 1 teaspoon dried parsley flakes
> 4 cups (two 16-ounce cans) sliced carrots, rinsed and drained
> 2 tablespoons Hormel Bacon Bits

In a large skillet sprayed with butter-flavored cooking spray, sauté onion for 5 minutes or until tender. Add tomato sauce, water, lemon pepper, Brown Sugar Twin, Sugar Twin, and parsley flakes. Mix well to combine. Bring mixture to a boil. Lower heat. Stir in carrots and bacon bits. Cover and simmer for 15 minutes, stirring occasionally.

Each serving equals:

HE: 2⅔ Vegetable • 12 Optional Calories

56 Calories • 0 gm Fat • 3 gm Protein •
11 gm Carbohydrate • 517 mg Sodium • 3 gm Fiber

DIABETIC: 2 Vegetable

Macaroni-Ham Skillet

● Serves 6

½ cup chopped onion

1 full cup (6 ounces) diced Dubuque 97% fat-free ham or any extra-lean ham

½ cup (one 2.5-ounce jar) sliced mushrooms, drained

3 cups hot cooked elbow macaroni, rinsed and drained

1 (10¾-ounce) can Healthy Request Cream of Mushroom Soup

½ cup skim milk

1 teaspoon dried parsley flakes

¼ cup (¾ ounce) grated Kraft fat-free Parmesan cheese

3 (¾-ounce) slices Kraft reduced-fat Swiss cheese

In a large skillet sprayed with butter-flavored cooking spray, sauté onion and ham for 5 minutes or until onion is tender. Stir in mushrooms and macaroni. Add mushroom soup, skim milk, parsley flakes, and Parmesan cheese. Mix well to combine. Lower heat and simmer for 5 minutes. Cut Swiss cheese slices in half. Evenly space cheese pieces over top of macaroni mixture. Cover and continue simmering for 2 to 3 minutes or until cheese melts. Divide into 6 (1-cup) servings.

HINT: 2 cups uncooked macaroni usually cooks to about 3 cups.

Each serving equals:

HE: 2 Protein • 1 Bread • ⅓ Vegetable • ¼ Slider • 15 Optional Calories

191 Calories • 3 gm Fat • 12 gm Protein • 29 gm Carbohydrate • 573 mg Sodium • 2 gm Fiber

DIABETIC: 2 Starch • 1½ Meat

Cherry Cola Cheesecake ❄

● Serves 8

2 (8-ounce) packages Philadelphia fat-free cream cheese
1 (4-serving) package JELL-O sugar-free instant vanilla pudding
    mix
⅔ cup Carnation Nonfat Dry Milk Powder
1 cup Diet Coke
¾ cup Cool Whip Lite☆
1 (6-ounce) Keebler graham cracker piecrust
½ cup cherry spreadable fruit spread
2 tablespoons (½ ounce) chopped pecans

In a large bowl, stir cream cheese with a spoon until soft. Add dry pudding mix, dry milk powder, and Diet Coke. Mix well using a wire whisk. Blend in ¼ cup Cool Whip Lite. Spread mixture evenly into piecrust. In a small bowl, combine remaining ½ cup Cool Whip Lite and cherry spreadable fruit. Spread topping mixture evenly over set filling. Evenly sprinkle pecans over top. Refrigerate for at least 20 minutes. Cut into 8 servings.

HINT: Spreadable fruit spreads best at room temperature.

Each serving equals:

HE: 1 Protein • 1 Fruit • ½ Bread • ¼ Skim Milk •
¼ Fat • ¾ Slider • 18 Optional Calories

251 Calories • 7 gm Fat • 11 gm Protein •
36 gm Carbohydrate • 686 mg Sodium • 0 gm Fiber

DIABETIC: 1 Meat • 1 Fruit • 1 Starch • 1 Fat

Menu 26

Chunky Carrot Salad
Deli-Style Ham and Veggie Pizza
Turtle Pie
Lemon Orange Ade

If you've never made your own pizza, you're about to don your chef's hat and try your wings! This recipe for deli-style pizza looks even better than the store-bought kind, and when you add ham to all those delectable veggies, you've got a meal that everyone will love! Serve your piping hot pizza and lively carrot salad with a tall glass of my Lemon Orange Ade, then finish the meal with fireworks in the form of a dazzling pie. Chocolate chips, pecans, and caramel as part of a healthy pie? I promised you pleasurable eating, and I always keep my promises!

Chunky Carrot Salad

○ Serves 8 (⅔ cup)

4 cups shredded carrots
1 cup (one 8-ounce can) pineapple chunks, packed in fruit juice,
    drained, and 2 tablespoons liquid reserved
½ cup raisins
1 cup chopped celery
⅔ cup Kraft fat-free mayonnaise
Sugar substitute to equal 1 tablespoon sugar

In a large bowl, combine carrots, pineapple, raisins, and celery. In a small bowl, combine mayonnaise, sugar substitute, and reserved pineapple liquid. Add mayonnaise mixture to carrot mixture. Mix well to combine. Cover and refrigerate for at least 20 minutes. Gently stir again just before serving.

HINT: To plump up raisins without "cooking," place in glass measuring cup and microwave on HIGH for 20 seconds.

Each serving equals:

HE: 1¼ Vegetable • ¾ Fruit • 14 Optional Calories

88 Calories • 0 gm Fat • 1 gm Protein •
21 gm Carbohydrate • 166 mg Sodium • 2 gm Fiber

DIABETIC: 1 Vegetable • 1 Fruit

Deli-Style Ham and Veggie Pizza

○ Serves 8

1 (11-ounce) can Pillsbury refrigerated crusty French loaf
2 tablespoons prepared mustard
2 full cups (12 ounces) finely diced Dubuque 97% fat-free ham or
     any extra-lean ham
½ cup chopped onion
¾ cup chopped green bell pepper
1½ cups peeled diced fresh tomato
1¼ cups chopped fresh mushrooms
1½ cups (6 ounces) shredded Kraft reduced-fat mozzarella
     cheese
2 teaspoons dried parsley flakes

Preheat oven to 375 degrees. Spray a rimmed 9-by-13-inch cookie sheet with butter-flavored cooking spray. Unroll French loaf and pat dough into prepared pan and up the sides to form a rim. Bake for 8 minutes or until light golden brown. Remove from oven. Evenly spread mustard over partially baked crust. Layer ham, onion, green pepper, tomato, and mushrooms over crust. Sprinkle mozzarella cheese and parsley flakes evenly over top. Bake for 15 minutes or until crust is golden and cheese is bubbly. Cut into 8 servings.

Each serving equals:

HE: 2 Protein • 1 Bread • 1 Vegetable

193 Calories • 5 gm Fat • 18 gm Protein •
19 gm Carbohydrate • 852 mg Sodium • 1 gm Fiber

DIABETIC: 2 Meat • 1 Starch • 1 Vegetable

Turtle Pie

❍ Serves 8

*1 (4-serving) package JELL-O sugar-free instant chocolate
    pudding mix*
⅔ cup Carnation Nonfat Dry Milk Powder
1¼ cups water
¾ cup Cool Whip Lite☆
¼ cup (1 ounce) chopped pecans☆
1 (6-ounce) Keebler graham cracker piecrust
1 tablespoon (¼ ounce) mini chocolate chips
1 tablespoon caramel sauce

In a large bowl, combine dry pudding mix, dry milk powder,
and water. Mix well using a wire whisk. Blend in ¼ cup Cool Whip
Lite. Stir in 2 tablespoons pecans. Spread mixture evenly into piecrust. Evenly spread remaining ½ cup Cool Whip Lite over pudding
mixture. Sprinkle chocolate chips and remaining 2 tablespoons pecans over top. Refrigerate for at least 20 minutes. Just before serving,
drizzle caramel sauce over top. Cut into 8 servings.

Each serving equals:

HE: ½ Bread • ½ Fat • ¼ Skim Milk • 1 Slider •
8 Optional Calories

188 Calories • 8 gm Fat • 4 gm Protein •
25 gm Carbohydrate • 340 mg Sodium • 1 gm Fiber

DIABETIC: 1½ Starch *or* Carbohydrate • 1 Fat

Lemon Orange Ade

○ Serves 8 (1 cup)

1 tub Crystal Light sugar-free lemonade mix
8 cups water
¼ of an orange cut into chunks, including skin and seeds

In a large pitcher, combine dry lemonade mix and water. Mix well using a long spoon. Pour 2 cups of prepared lemonade into blender; add orange chunks and blend on HIGH for 30 to 45 seconds. Pour back into the pitcher of lemonade mixture and mix well. Serve over ice.

Each serving equals:

HE: 1 Optional Calorie

0 Calories • 0 gm Fat • 0 gm Protein •
0 gm Carbohydrate • 0 mg Sodium • 0 gm Fiber

DIABETIC: Free Food

Menu 27

California Ranch Corn Salad
Sour Cream Cabbage
Busy Day Pork Casserole
Heavenly Orange Fluff

Cliff enjoys corn as much as I do, so I stir it into lots of favorite recipes, like this rainbow-colored corn salad. It's a nice contrast in color and texture to a creamy cabbage dish that tastes anything but "diet." I've selected pork tenderloins for this menu's entree; it's a lean and luscious way to enjoy one of our best-loved meats. If you're a fan of the dessert salad called ambrosia, you'll find that my light, fruity fluff is delectable enough to serve at a banquet!

California Ranch Corn Salad

● Serves 4 (¾ cup)

> 2 cups frozen whole kernel corn, thawed
> 1 cup diced fresh tomato
> ½ cup diced green bell pepper
> ¼ cup diced onion
> ¼ cup finely chopped fresh parsley
> 3 tablespoons Kraft Fat Free Ranch Dressing
> 1 tablespoon Kraft fat-free mayonnaise
> Sugar substitute to equal 1 teaspoon sugar
> ¼ teaspoon black pepper

In a medium bowl, combine corn, tomato, green pepper, onion, and parsley. In a small bowl, combine Ranch dressing, mayonnaise, sugar substitute, and black pepper. Add dressing mixture to corn mixture. Mix well to combine. Cover and refrigerate for at least 20 minutes. Gently stir again just before serving.

HINT: Thaw corn by placing in a colander and rinsing with hot water for one minute.

Each serving equals:

HE: 1 Bread • 1 Vegetable • ¼ Slider •
2 Optional Calories

112 Calories • 0 gm Fat • 3 gm Protein •
25 gm Carbohydrate • 154 mg Sodium • 3 gm Fiber

DIABETIC: 1 Starch • 1 Vegetable

Sour Cream Cabbage

○ Serves 4 (1 cup)

6 cups shredded cabbage
2 tablespoons water
¼ cup Land O Lakes no-fat sour cream
1 tablespoon white vinegar
½ teaspoon lemon pepper

In a large skillet sprayed with butter-flavored cooking spray, combine cabbage and water. Cover and cook on low heat for 8 minutes or just until soft. In a small bowl, combine sour cream, vinegar, and lemon pepper. Add sour cream mixture to undrained cabbage mixture. Mix well to combine. Continue cooking for 2 to 3 minutes or until mixture is heated through.

HINT: Leftovers are as good or better the next day.

Each serving equals:

HE: 3 Vegetable • 15 Optional Calories

40 Calories • 0 gm Fat • 2 gm Protein •
8 gm Carbohydrate • 151 mg Sodium • 2 gm Fiber

DIABETIC: 2 Vegetable

Busy Day Pork Casserole

○ Serves 4

4 (4-ounce) lean tenderized pork tenderloins
1 (10¾-ounce) can Healthy Request Cream of Mushroom Soup
½ cup (one 2.5-ounce jar) sliced mushrooms, drained
2 cups (one 16-ounce can) cut green beans, rinsed and drained
¼ teaspoon lemon pepper
3 tablespoons (¾ ounce) dried fine bread crumbs

Preheat oven to 375 degrees. Spray an 8-by-8-inch baking dish with butter-flavored cooking spray. Lightly brown tenderloins in a large skillet sprayed with butter-flavored cooking spray. Place tenderloins in prepared baking dish. In same skillet, combine mushroom soup, mushrooms, green beans, and lemon pepper. Cook for 2 to 3 minutes, stirring often. Pour soup mixture evenly over browned meat. Sprinkle bread crumbs evenly over the top. Bake for 20 minutes, or until pork is tender. Divide into 4 servings.

Each serving equals:

HE: 3 Protein • 1¼ Vegetable • ¼ Bread • ½ Slider • 1 Optional Calorie

227 Calories • 7 gm Fat • 27 gm Protein • 14 gm Carbohydrate • 516 mg Sodium • 1 gm Fiber

DIABETIC: 3 Meat • 1 Vegetable • ½ Starch

Heavenly Orange Fluff

⊙ Serves 6

¾ cup Yoplait plain fat-free yogurt
1 cup Carnation Nonfat Dry Milk Powder ☆
Sugar substitute to equal 2 tablespoons sugar
1 teaspoon coconut extract
¾ cup Cool Whip Lite
1 (4-serving) package JELL-O sugar-free orange gelatin
1 (4-serving) package JELL-O sugar-free instant vanilla pudding
*   mix*
1 cup Diet Mountain Dew
1 cup (one 8-ounce can) crushed pineapple, packed in fruit juice,
*   undrained*
1 cup (one 11-ounce can) mandarin oranges, rinsed and drained
2 tablespoons flaked coconut

In a small bowl, combine yogurt and ⅓ cup dry milk powder.
Add sugar substitute and coconut extract. Mix well to combine. Stir
in Cool Whip Lite. Set aside. In a large bowl, combine dry gelatin,
dry pudding mix, and remaining ⅔ cup dry milk powder. Add Diet
Mountain Dew and undrained pineapple. Mix well using a wire
whisk. Fold yogurt mixture into pudding mixture. Add mandarin
oranges. Mix gently to combine. Evenly spoon mixture into 6 dessert dishes. Top each with 1 teaspoon coconut. Refrigerate for at
least 20 minutes.

HINT: Diet 7-UP or water may be used in place of Diet Mountain
Dew.

Each serving equals:

HE: ⅔ Fruit • ⅔ Skim Milk • ½ Slider •
10 Optional Calories

141 Calories • 1 gm Fat • 7 gm Protein •
26 gm Carbohydrate • 353 mg Sodium • 0 gm Fiber

DIABETIC: 1 Fruit • 1 Skim Milk

Menu 28

Carrot-Pea Salad
Old-Fashioned Apple Salad
Tomato Pork Stroganoff
Apple-Cranberry Cider

Here's another good way to serve pork, in a scrumptious stroganoff that tastes forbidden—and, according to my taste tester, Cliff—fantastic! Partnered with a pretty blend of peas and carrots plus a nutty-crunchy classic Waldorf salad, this is a meal your family will request again and again. I've included a wonderful homemade cider blend that's perfect for cool nights in early fall, but easy enough to fix anytime at all. It'll warm your heart and your soul!

Carrot-Pea Salad

○ Serves 4 (full ½ cup)

> *¼ cup Kraft Fat Free Ranch Dressing*
> *2 tablespoons Kraft fat-free mayonnaise*
> *2 teaspoons dried onion flakes*
> *1 teaspoon dried parsley flakes*
> *1 teaspoon lemon juice*
> *Sugar substitute to equal 2 teaspoons sugar*
> *2 cups (one 16-ounce can) sliced carrots, rinsed and drained*
> *1½ cups frozen peas, thawed*

In a medium bowl, combine Ranch dressing, mayonnaise, onion flakes, parsley flakes, lemon juice, and sugar substitute. Add carrots and peas. Mix well to combine. Cover and refrigerate for at least 20 minutes. Gently stir again just before serving.

HINT: Thaw peas by placing in a colander and rinsing under hot water for one minute.

Each serving equals:

HE: 1 Vegetable • ¾ Bread • ¼ Slider •
11 Optional Calories

96 Calories • 0 gm Fat • 4 gm Protein •
20 gm Carbohydrate • 260 mg Sodium • 6 gm Fiber

DIABETIC: 1 Vegetable • 1 Starch

Old-Fashioned Apple Salad

● Serves 4 (¾ cup)

2 cups (4 small) cored, unpeeled, and diced Red Delicious apples
¼ cup raisins
¼ cup (1 ounce) chopped walnuts
½ cup Cool Whip Lite
2 tablespoons Kraft fat-free mayonnaise
1 teaspoon lemon juice
½ teaspoon apple pie spice

In a medium bowl, combine apples, raisins, and walnuts. In a small bowl, combine Cool Whip Lite, mayonnaise, lemon juice, and apple pie spice. Add Cool Whip Lite mixture to apple mixture. Mix gently to combine. Cover and refrigerate for at least 20 minutes. Gently stir again just before serving.

HINT: To plump up raisins without "cooking," place in a glass measuring cup and microwave on HIGH 20 seconds.

Each serving equals:

HE: 1½ Fruit • ½ Fat • ¼ Protein • ¼ Slider • 5 Optional Calories

129 Calories • 5 gm Fat • 1 gm Protein • 20 gm Carbohydrate • 55 mg Sodium • 2 gm Fiber

DIABETIC: 1½ Fruit • 1 Fat

Tomato Pork Stroganoff ❄

○ Serves 4 (1 cup)

1 cup chopped onion
½ cup (one 2.5-ounce jar) sliced mushrooms, drained
1 full cup (6 ounces) diced lean cooked roast pork
1 (10¾-ounce) can Healthy Request Tomato Soup
1 teaspoon dried parsley flakes
¼ teaspoon black pepper
¼ cup Land O Lakes no-fat sour cream
2 cups hot cooked noodles, rinsed and drained

In a large skillet sprayed with butter-flavored cooking spray, sauté onion for 5 minutes or until tender. Add mushrooms, roast pork, tomato soup, parsley flakes, and black pepper. Mix well to combine. Stir in sour cream and noodles. Lower heat and simmer for 5 minutes or until mixture is heated through, stirring often.

HINTS: 1. If you don't have leftovers, purchase a chunk of cooked roast pork from your local deli.

2. Lean roast beef may be used in place of pork.

3. 1¾ cups uncooked noodles usually cooks to about 2 cups.

Each serving equals:

HE: 1½ Protein • 1 Bread • ¾ Vegetable • ¾ Slider

278 Calories • 6 gm Fat • 18 gm Protein •
38 mg Carbohydrate • 428 mg Sodium • 6 gm Fiber

DIABETIC: 2 Starch • 1½ Meat • 1 Vegetable

Apple-Cranberry Cider

◑ Serves 4 (1 cup)

1½ cups unsweetened apple juice
1¾ cups Diet 7-UP
1 cup Ocean Spray reduced-calorie cranberry juice cocktail
1 teaspoon apple pie spice

In a medium saucepan, combine apple juice, Diet 7-UP, and
cranberry juice. Add apple pie spice. Mix well to combine. Simmer
for 15 minutes, stirring occasionally.

Each serving equals:

HE: 1 Fruit

56 Calories • 0 gm Fat • 0 gm Protein •
14 gm Carbohydrate • 29 mg Sodium • 0 gm Fiber

DIABETIC: 1 Fruit

Menu 29

Veggie Coleslaw
Festive Pea Salad
Hot Roast Beef Sandwiches
Queen Anne's Cheesecake

You can never have too many spirited salads and slaws in your repertoire, so here are a couple more good ones. The first incorporates green pepper and zucchini with the traditional coleslaw blend, while the second surprises with the crunch of cashews and a tangy-spicy mustard-mayo dressing. I tend to like serving some crunchy salads with an old family favorite like hot roast beef sandwiches with rich gravy—it makes for a lively contrast. Just leave room for a pineapple cherry cheesecake that's fit for a queen!

Veggie Coleslaw

○ Serves 4 (1 full cup)

½ cup Kraft fat-free mayonnaise
¼ teaspoon black pepper
1 teaspoon Italian seasoning
2 cups shredded cabbage
½ cup shredded carrots
¼ cup finely diced green bell pepper
¾ cup shredded zucchini

In a large bowl, combine mayonnaise, black pepper, and Italian seasoning. Add cabbage, carrots, green pepper, and zucchini. Mix well to combine. Cover and refrigerate for at least 20 minutes. Gently stir again just before serving.

HINT: 2½ cups purchased coleslaw mix may be substituted for cabbage and carrots.

Each serving equals:

HE: 1¾ Vegetable • ¼ Slider

36 Calories • 0 gm Fat • 1 gm Protein •
8 gm Carbohydrate • 222 mg Sodium • 1 gm Fiber

DIABETIC: 1 Vegetable • 1 Free Vegetable

Festive Pea Salad

○ Serves 4 (¾ cup)

2 cups frozen peas, thawed
¼ cup chopped green onion
½ cup chopped celery
¾ cup chopped fresh cauliflower
¼ cup (1 ounce) chopped cashews
½ cup Kraft fat-free mayonnaise
1 teaspoon prepared mustard
Sugar substitute to equal 2 teaspoons sugar
1 hard-boiled egg, chopped

In a large bowl, combine peas, green onion, celery, cauliflower, and cashews. In a small bowl, combine mayonnaise, mustard, and sugar substitute. Add mayonnaise mixture to vegetable mixture. Mix well to combine. Fold in egg. Cover and refrigerate for at least 20 minutes. Gently stir again just before serving.

HINTS: 1. Thaw peas by placing in a colander and rinsing with hot water for one minute.

2. If you want the look and feel of eggs without the cholesterol, toss out the yolk and dice the white.

Each serving equals:

HE: 1 Bread • ¾ Vegetable • ½ Fat •
½ Protein (¼ limited) • ¼ Slider • 1 Optional Calorie

149 Calories • 5 gm Fat • 7 gm Protein •
19 gm Carbohydrate • 239 mg Sodium • 5 gm Fiber

DIABETIC: 1 Starch • 1 Vegetable • 1 Fat

Hot Roast Beef Sandwiches

○ Serves 4

1 (6-ounce) package Healthy Choice sliced 97% fat-free roast
   beef
1 (12-ounce) jar Heinz Fat Free Beef Gravy
1⅔ cups hot water
1⅓ cups (3 ounces) instant potato flakes
⅓ cup Carnation Nonfat Dry Milk Powder
1 teaspoon dried parsley flakes
¼ teaspoon black pepper
8 slices reduced-calorie white bread

Place roast beef in microwave and microwave on BAKE (60%
power) for 2 minutes. Meanwhile, in a small saucepan, warm gravy.
Also, in a medium saucepan, bring water to a boil. Remove water
from heat. Stir in potato flakes, dry milk powder, parsley flakes,
and black pepper. Mix well using a fork. For each serving, place 1
slice bread on plate, arrange ¼ of the roast beef slices over the bread,
and top with another slice of bread; cut in half, spoon about ½ cup
mashed potatoes in center of each sandwich and spoon about ⅓
cup gravy over top.

Each serving equals:

HE: 2 Bread • 1 Protein • ¼ Skim Milk • ¼ Slider •
18 Optional Calories

---

221 Calories • 1 gm Fat • 19 gm Protein •
34 gm Carbohydrate • 976 mg Sodium • 1 gm Fiber

DIABETIC: 2½ Starch • 1 Meat

Queen Anne's Cheesecake

● Serves 8

> 2 (8-ounce) packages Philadelphia fat-free cream cheese
> 1 (4-serving) package JELL-O sugar-free instant vanilla pudding
> mix
> 1 (4-serving) package JELL-O sugar-free cherry gelatin
> ⅔ cup Carnation Nonfat Dry Milk Powder
> 1 cup (one 8-ounce can) crushed pineapple, packed in fruit juice,
> undrained
> ¼ cup water
> 8 maraschino cherries, quartered
> ¾ cup Cool Whip Lite ☆
> 1 (6-ounce) Keebler graham cracker piecrust

In a large bowl, stir cream cheese with a spoon until soft. Add dry pudding mix, dry gelatin, dry milk powder, undrained pineapple, and water. Mix well using a wire whisk. Reserve 8 cherry pieces. Gently fold remaining cherry pieces and ¼ cup Cool Whip Lite into pudding mixture. Spread mixture evenly into piecrust. Refrigerate for at least 20 minutes. Cut into 8 servings. When serving, top each piece with 1 tablespoon Cool Whip Lite and garnish with 1 piece of reserved cherry.

Each serving equals:

HE: 1 Protein • ½ Bread • ¼ Fruit • ¼ Skim Milk •
1 Slider • 13 Optional Calories

226 Calories • 6 gm Fat • 12 gm Protein •
31 gm Carbohydrate • 698 mg Sodium • 1 gm Fiber

DIABETIC: 2 Starch *or* Carbohydrate • 1 Meat • 1 Fat

Menu 30

Old-Time Spinach Salad
Tomato and Cucumber Macaroni Salad
Quick BBQ Beef Sandwiches
Strawberry Lover's Pudding Treats

A classic's a classic whether it's served traditional style or reinvented for healthy appetites and healthy hearts! If you're surprised to see barbecued beef in a healthy cookbook, don't be—beef provides lots of great nutrition when combined with other good-for-you ingredients, and husbands and kids love it too much to give it up. This is a meal full of classics with a healthy twist—a true spinach salad with real bacon, a hearty macaroni salad blended with cheese, barbecued beef with the flavor of the real thing, and a rich-tasting dessert to top it off. Couldn't you eat this way for a lifetime? I knew it!

Old-Time Spinach Salad

◐ Serves 4 (1⅓ cups)

> 4 cups fresh torn spinach leaves, stems discarded
> 1 hard-boiled egg, chopped
> 2 tablespoons Hormel Bacon Bits
> 1 cup sliced fresh mushrooms
> ½ cup Kraft Fat Free French Dressing
> 1 tablespoon finely chopped onion
> ½ teaspoon Worcestershire sauce
> 1 tablespoon Brown Sugar Twin

In a medium bowl, combine spinach, egg, bacon bits, and mushrooms. In a small bowl, combine French dressing, onion, Worcestershire sauce, and Brown Sugar Twin. Add dressing mixture to spinach mixture. Toss well to coat. Serve at once.

HINT: If you want the look and feel of eggs without the cholesterol, toss out the yolk and dice the white.

Each serving equals:

HE: 2½ Vegetable • ¼ Protein (limited) • ¼ Slider • 19 Optional Calories

90 Calories • 2 gm Fat • 5 gm Protein • 13 gm Carbohydrate • 375 mg Sodium • 2 gm Fiber

DIABETIC: 2 Vegetable • ½ Fat

Tomato and Cucumber Macaroni Salad

○ Serves 4 (1 cup)

> 2 cups cold cooked macaroni, rinsed and drained
> 1 cup chopped fresh tomatoes
> 1 cup unpeeled chopped cucumbers
> ¾ cup (3 ounces) shredded Kraft reduced-fat Cheddar cheese
> ½ cup Kraft Fat Free Catalina Dressing
> ¼ cup fat-free mayonnaise
> 2 teaspoons Dijon mustard
> 1 teaspoon dried onion flakes
> 1 tablespoon fresh parsley or 1 teaspoon dried parsley flakes

In a medium bowl, combine macaroni, tomatoes, cucumbers, and Cheddar cheese. In a small bowl, combine Catalina dressing, mayonnaise, Dijon mustard, onion flakes, and parsley. Add dressing mixture to pasta mixture. Mix gently to combine. Cover and refrigerate for at least 20 minutes. Gently stir again just before serving.

HINT: 1⅓ cups uncooked macaroni usually cooks to about 2 cups.

Each serving equals:

HE: 1 Bread • 1 Vegetable • 1 Protein • ¼ Slider • 15 Optional Calories

220 Calories • 4 gm Fat • 10 gm Protein • 36 gm Carbohydrate • 641 mg Sodium • 2 gm Fiber

DIABETIC: 2 Starch • 1 Vegetable • 1 Meat

Quick BBQ Beef Sandwiches ❄

○ Serves 4 (½ cup filling)

½ cup finely diced green bell pepper
½ cup finely chopped onion
1 (10¾-ounce) can Healthy Request Tomato Soup
1 tablespoon Brown Sugar Twin
1 tablespoon white vinegar
1 teaspoon Worcestershire sauce
1 (6-ounce) package Healthy Choice sliced 97% fat-free roast
    beef, shredded
4 reduced-calorie hamburger buns

In a large skillet sprayed with butter-flavored cooking spray, sauté green pepper and onion for 5 minutes or until tender. Stir in tomato soup, Brown Sugar Twin, vinegar, and Worcestershire sauce. Bring mixture to a boil. Add roast beef. Mix well to combine. Lower heat and simmer for 10 minutes, stirring occasionally. Serve on hamburger buns.

Each serving equals:

HE: 1 Protein • 1 Bread • ½ Vegetable • ½ Slider • 6 Optional Calories

187 Calories • 3 gm Fat • 11 gm Protein • 29 gm Carbohydrate • 817 mg Sodium • 4 gm Fiber

DIABETIC: 2 Starch • 1 Meat

Strawberry Lover's Pudding Treats

○ Serves 4

1 (4-serving) package JELL-O sugar-free instant vanilla pudding
    mix
1 (4-serving) package JELL-O sugar-free strawberry gelatin
⅔ cup Carnation Nonfat Dry Milk Powder
1 cup sliced fresh strawberries, mashed
¾ cup water
½ teaspoon vanilla extract
¼ cup Cool Whip Lite

In a medium bowl, combine dry pudding mix, dry gelatin, and dry milk powder. Add mashed strawberries and water. Mix well using a wire whisk. Blend in vanilla extract and Cool Whip Lite. Evenly spoon mixture into 4 dessert dishes. Refrigerate for at least 20 minutes.

Each serving equals:

HE: ½ Skim Milk • ¼ Fruit • ½ Slider •
5 Optional Calories

93 Calories • 1 gm Fat • 5 gm Protein •
16 gm Carbohydrate • 446 mg Sodium • 0 gm Fiber

DIABETIC: 1 Starch *or* Carbohydrate

Index of Recipes

I want to hear from you...

Besides my family, the love of my life is creating "common folk" healthy recipes and solving everyday cooking questions in *The Healthy Exchanges Way*. Everyone who uses my recipes is considered part of the Healthy Exchanges Family, so please write to me if you have any questions, comments, or suggestions. I will do my best to answer. With your support, I'll continue to stir up even more recipes and cooking tips for the Family in the years to come.

Write to: JoAnna M. Lund
c/o Healthy Exchanges, Inc.
P.O. Box 124
DeWitt, IA 52742

If you prefer, you can call me at 1-319-659-8234, fax me at 1-319-659-2126, or contact me via E-mail by writing to HealthyJo @aol.com.

Now that you've seen *30 Meals/30 Minutes,* why not order *The Healthy Exchanges Food Newsletter?*

If you enjoyed the recipes in this cookbook and would like to cook up even more of these "common folk" healthy dishes, you may want to subscribe to *The Healthy Exchanges Food Newsletter.*

This monthly 12-page newsletter contains 30-plus new recipes *every month* in such columns as:

- Reader Exchange
- Reader Requests
- Recipe Makeover
- Micro Corner
- Dinner for Two
- Crock Pot Luck
- Meatless Main Dishes
- Rise & Shine
- Our Small World
- Brown Bagging It
- Snack Attack
- Side Dishes
- Main Dishes
- Desserts

In addition to all the recipes, other regular features include:
- The Editor's Motivational Corner
- Dining Out Question & Answer
- Cooking Question & Answer
- New Product Alert
- Success Profiles of Winners in the Losing Game
- Exercise Advice from a Cardiac Rehab Specialist
- Nutrition Advice from a Registered Dietitian
- Positive Thought for the Month

Just as in this cookbook, all *Healthy Exchanges Food Newsletter* recipes are calculated in three distinct ways: 1) Weight Loss Choices, 2) Calories with Fat and Fiber Grams, and 3) Diabetic Exchanges.

The cost for a one-year (12-issue) subscription with a special Healthy Exchanges 3-ring binder to store the newsletters in is $27.50. To order, simply complete the form and mail to us *or* call our toll-free number and pay with your VISA or MasterCard.

_____ Yes, I want to subscribe to *The Healthy Exchanges Food Newsletter*. $27.50 Yearly Subscription Cost............................... $_____

_____ Foreign orders please add $6.00 for money exchange and extra postage.................. $_____

_____ I'm not sure, so please send me a sample copy at $2.50...................................... $_____

Please make check payable to HEALTHY EXCHANGES or pay by VISA/MasterCard

CARD NUMBER:_____ EXPIRATION DATE:_____

SIGNATURE:_____

Signature required for all credit card orders.

Or order toll-free, using your credit card, at 1-800-766-8961

NAME: _____

ADDRESS: _____

CITY _____ STATE _____ ZIP _____

TELEPHONE: ( ) _____

If additional orders for the newsletter are to be sent to an address other than the one listed above, please use a separate sheet and attach to this form.

MAIL TO: **HEALTHY EXCHANGES**
P.O. BOX 124
DeWitt, IA 52742-0124

1-800-766-8961 For Customer Orders
1-319-659-8234 For Customer Service

Thank you for your order, and for choosing to become a part of the Healthy Exchanges Family!

About the Author

JoAnna M. Lund is the author of *Healthy Exchanges Cookbook; HELP: Healthy Exchanges Lifetime Plan*; and *The Diabetic's Healthy Exchanges Cookbook*. She has been profiled in national and local publications, including *People, The New York Times, Forbes,* and *The National Enquirer,* and has appeared on hundreds of radio and television shows. A popular speaker with weight loss, cardiac, and diabetic support groups, she can be seen weekly on public television with her show *Help Yourself with JoAnna Lund.*